ANCIENT CHINA

Tony Allan

CHELSEA HOUSE
PUBLISHERS

An imprint of Infobase Publishing

Cultural Atlas for Young People
ANCIENT CHINA
First Edition

Copyright © 2007 The Brown Reference Group plc

Chelsea House
An imprint of Infobase Publishing
132 West 31st Street
New York, NY 10001

Library of Congress Cataloging-in-Publication Data available upon request.

ISBN: 0-8160-6827-5

ISBN 13 digit: 978-0-8160-6827-2

Set ISBN: 978-0-8160-7218-7

Chelsea House books are available at special discounts when purchased in bulk quantities for businesses, associations, institutions, or sales promotions. Please call our Special Sales Department in New York at (212) 967-8800 or (800) 322-8755.

You can find Chelsea House on the World Wide Web at:
http://www.chelseahouse.com

The Brown Reference Group
(incorporating Andromeda Oxford Limited)
8 Chapel Place, Rivington Street
London EC2Λ 3DQ
www.brownreference.com

For The Brown Reference Group:
Editorial Director: Lindsey Lowe
Project Editor: Graham Bateman
Editor: Virginia Carter
Design: Steve McCurdy
Senior Managing Editor: Tim Cooke

Printed in Singapore

10 9 8 7 6 5 4 3 2 1

Contents

Introduction

I N TERMS OF CULTURAL CONTINUITY, CHINA IS THE WORLD'S OLDEST living civilization. Almost 4,000 years have passed since the emergence of the first historically recorded dynasty, the Shang. Over the centuries, the nation has known contrasting fortunes. It has alternately been divided into rival kingdoms and unified as a single bureaucratic state. It has been ruled by indigenous Chinese and fallen to invading dynasties from the west and north. It has waged aggressive campaigns of imperial expansion but also experienced centuries when it turned inward, minimizing contact with the rest of the world. It has gloried in its role as the Middle Kingdom, the center of world civilization, yet has also known times of humiliation at the hands of its neighbors and the great powers of the West.

Throughout its long history, however, China has retained its cultural and artistic identity, developing unique forms of architecture, poetry, painting, calligraphy, and theater. It has its own distinctive patterns of thought, shaped by Confucianism and Daoism—philosophical systems that originated more than two millennia ago and that still have an influence today.

Chinese society too remains individual, dynamic, and contradictory. In the countryside there are farmers still living a life not hugely different from that which their peasant ancestors knew a thousand years ago; yet in China's booming cities, investment and industrialization are transforming the lives of millions of residents and creating an economic powerhouse for the 21st century.

This book concentrates on the long historical hinterland that has helped shape China today. The first part tells the story of the nation's history from its beginnings up to the collapse of the Ming Dynasty in 1644. Dynasties loom large in the telling, for in a nation with as lengthy a historical shadow as China's, lines of rulers have themselves come and gone, leaving their names as markers for successive ages: the Han era, the Tang centuries, the Song years, and the Ming epoch.

Their rise and fall has followed a cyclical pattern that has seen long-lasting lines eventually brought down by structural weaknesses. Sometimes the problem was economic; government revenues failed to match spending, or excessive taxation choked off the nation's productive capacity. More than once the fault lay in the remoteness of the emperors from the subjects they governed—cocooned in luxury as they often were in a narrow world, living with eunuchs and concubines.

On occasion nature played a part, spreading famine as a result of droughts or floods. Often all of these factors and others too came together to cause a dynasty's decline. Then a time of troubles would follow in which the nation fractured into rival kingdoms, and competing warlords jostled for power. Eventually a strong leader would emerge to impose his will on all his rivals and reunite the nation once more. Then a fresh dynasty would be installed, setting off the cycle once more.

Yet while dynasties rose and fell, other aspects of life went on regardless. The second part of the book focuses on the continuities of Chinese culture and society, from the landscape, the countryside, and rice cultivation to medicine, technology, and the arts. This section also highlights some spectacular survivals from China's past: the underground army of terra-cotta warriors buried to protect the First Emperor's tomb; the Great Wall that guarded the nation's northern border, and the Forbidden City, built by the Ming emperors as an imperial enclave in the heart of their capital, Beijing. A glossary on pages 92–93 explains unfamiliar terms, while the Timelines on pages 6–7 list the key events that have shaped China's history, along with the dates when they occurred.

Ancient China provides a succinct introduction to one of the world's great civilizations. The story it tells is all the more important because, unlike many of the great early civilizations, China continues to play a major part in shaping the world today.

Abbreviations used in this book

B.C.E. = Before Common Era (also known as B.C.).
C.E. = Common Era (also known as A.D.). c. = *circa* (about).
in = inch; yd = yard; ft = foot; mi = mile.
cm = centimeter; m = meter; km = kilometer.

▶ The teachings of the philosopher Confucius have had a profound influence on Chinese life and thought for more than 2,500 years.

Timelines

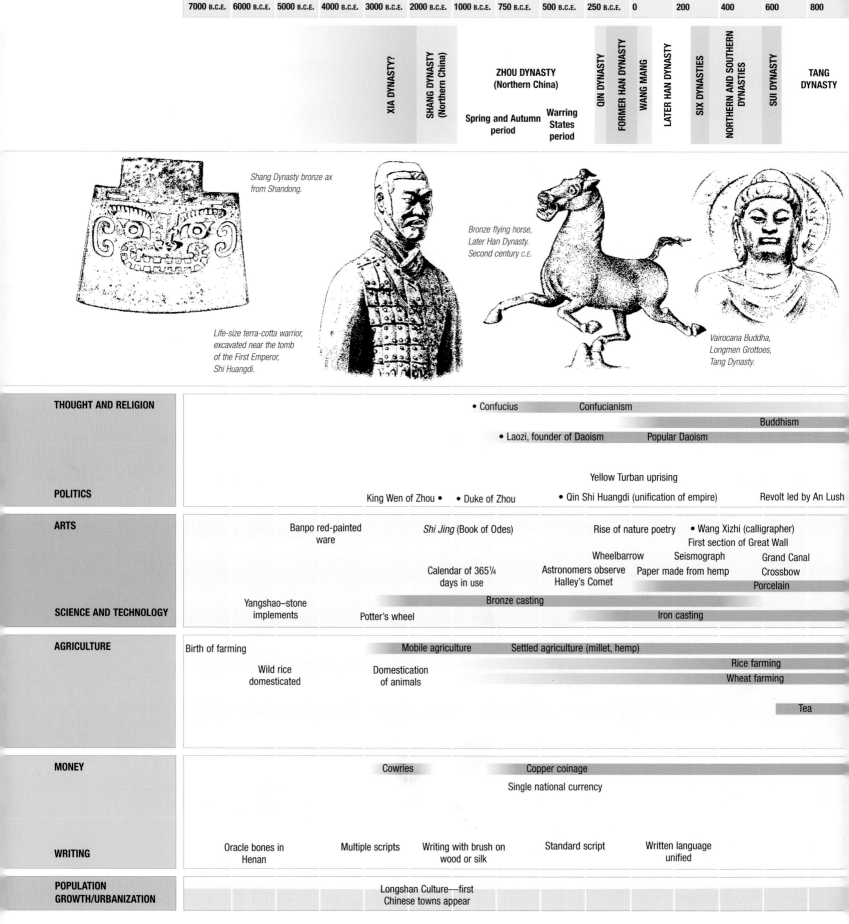

| | 7000 B.C.E. | 6000 B.C.E. | 5000 B.C.E. | 4000 B.C.E. | 3000 B.C.E. | 2000 B.C.E. | 1000 B.C.E. | 750 B.C.E. | 500 B.C.E. | 250 B.C.E. | 0 | 200 | 400 | 600 | 800 |

Dynasties: XIA DYNASTY? · SHANG DYNASTY (Northern China) · ZHOU DYNASTY (Northern China) [Spring and Autumn period / Warring States period] · QIN DYNASTY · FORMER HAN DYNASTY · WANG MANG · LATER HAN DYNASTY · SIX DYNASTIES · NORTHERN AND SOUTHERN DYNASTIES · SUI DYNASTY · TANG DYNASTY

Shang Dynasty bronze ax from Shandong.

Life-size terra-cotta warrior, excavated near the tomb of the First Emperor, Shi Huangdi.

Bronze flying horse, Later Han Dynasty. Second century C.E.

Vairocana Buddha, Longmen Grottoes, Tang Dynasty.

THOUGHT AND RELIGION
- Confucius · Confucianism
- Buddhism
- Laozi, founder of Daoism · Popular Daoism

POLITICS
- Yellow Turban uprising
- King Wen of Zhou · Duke of Zhou · Qin Shi Huangdi (unification of empire) · Revolt led by An Lush

ARTS
- Banpo red-painted ware
- Shi Jing (Book of Odes)
- Rise of nature poetry · Wang Xizhi (calligrapher)
- First section of Great Wall

SCIENCE AND TECHNOLOGY
- Wheelbarrow · Seismograph · Grand Canal
- Calendar of 365¼ days in use · Astronomers observe Halley's Comet · Paper made from hemp · Crossbow
- Porcelain
- Bronze casting
- Yangshao—stone implements · Potter's wheel · Iron casting

AGRICULTURE
- Birth of farming · Mobile agriculture · Settled agriculture (millet, hemp)
- Rice farming
- Wild rice domesticated · Domestication of animals · Wheat farming
- Tea

MONEY
- Cowries · Copper coinage
- Single national currency

WRITING
- Oracle bones in Henan · Multiple scripts · Writing with brush on wood or silk · Standard script · Written language unified

POPULATION GROWTH/URBANIZATION
- Longshan Culture—first Chinese towns appear

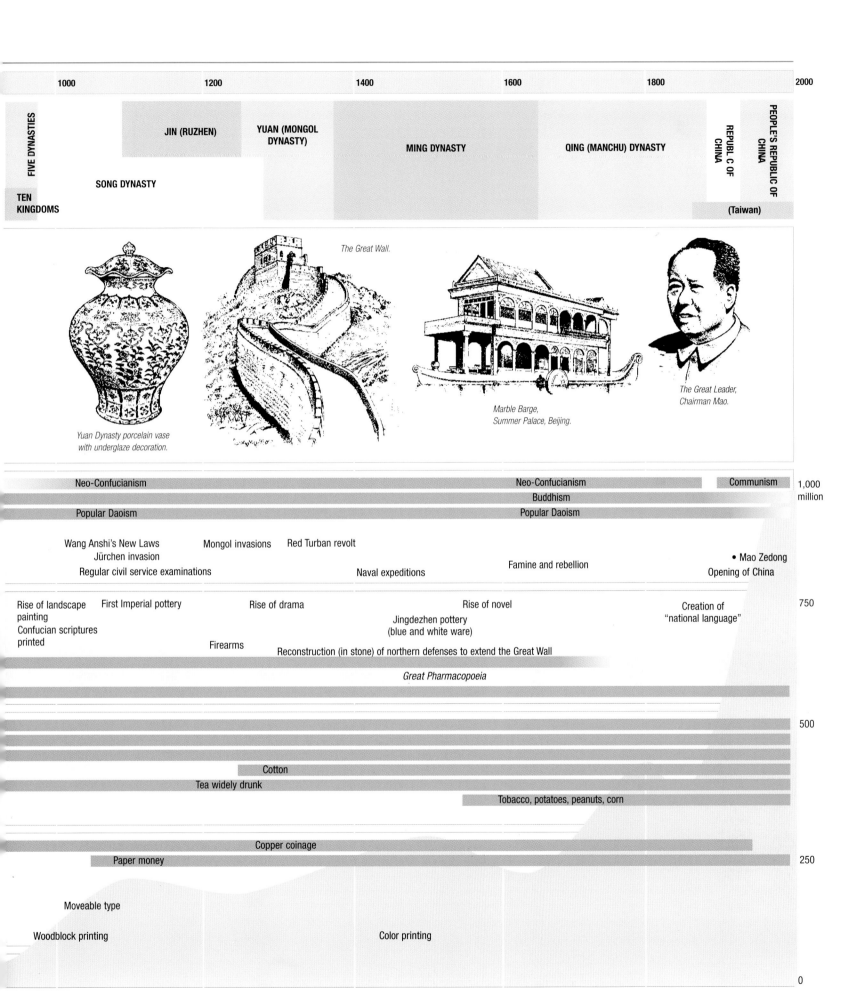

1000	1200	1400	1600	1800	2000

FIVE DYNASTIES

JIN (RUZHEN)

YUAN (MONGOL DYNASTY)

MING DYNASTY

QING (MANCHU) DYNASTY

REPUBLIC OF CHINA

PEOPLE'S REPUBLIC OF CHINA

SONG DYNASTY

TEN KINGDOMS

(Taiwan)

The Great Wall.

Yuan Dynasty porcelain vase with underglaze decoration.

Marble Barge, Summer Palace, Beijing.

The Great Leader, Chairman Mao.

Neo-Confucianism   Neo-Confucianism   Communism   1,000 million

Buddhism

Popular Daoism   Popular Daoism

Wang Anshi's New Laws   Mongol invasions   Red Turban revolt
Jürchen invasion
                                                          Famine and rebellion   • Mao Zedong
Regular civil service examinations   Naval expeditions   Opening of China

Rise of landscape   First Imperial pottery   Rise of drama   Rise of novel   Creation of   750
painting   "national language"
                                              Jingdezhen pottery
Confucian scriptures   (blue and white ware)
printed
                    Firearms   Reconstruction (in stone) of northern defenses to extend the Great Wall

Great Pharmacopoeia

500

Cotton

Tea widely drunk

Tobacco, potatoes, peanuts, corn

Copper coinage

Paper money   250

Moveable type

Woodblock printing   Color printing

0

Part One

The History
of China

▲ This carved figure is one of the statues lining the approach to the Ming Tombs near Beijing. The Ming Dynasty was the last native Chinese dynasty to rule the empire and spanned almost 300 years from the late 14th to mid-17th centuries.

▶ A 19th-century print representing the life of the Chinese emperors. Many Chinese emperors were strong rulers surrounded by courtiers, who all enjoyed a life of privilege.

Prehistoric China

CHINA WAS INHABITED FROM THE EARLIEST times. In caves at Zhoukoudian, about 30 miles (50 km) from Beijing, archaeologists have found bones 460,000 years old. The remains were those of *Homo erectus*, an ancestor of *Homo sapiens*, the modern human. Named "Beijing Man," these prehumans made tools from flint and quartz and hunted wild animals, mostly deer. Ash found on the cave floors suggests that they already knew how to control fire. More recent finds of stone tools at Renzidong in Anhui province are thought to date back possibly as far as 2.25 million years.

Other caverns in the Zhoukoudian complex were in use as recently as 10,000 years ago, by which time their occupants had long been modern humans (*Homo sapiens*). Scholars argue about whether they evolved from China's earlier *Homo erectus* population or if they emigrated separately from Africa, where *Homo sapiens* is thought to have begun. Whatever their origins, they lived much like their *Homo erectus* predecessors—hunting, fishing, and gathering wild fruits and berries in the surrounding countryside.

Origins of farming

Farming reached China in about 7000 B.C.E. As elsewhere in the world, it first appeared in the great river valleys. In China's case that meant the Yellow (Huang) River, which flows through a landscape of loess—a crumbly soil blown by winds from the Gobi Desert 600 miles (1,000 km) away. Rich in minerals, the loess, whose yellow silt gave the river its name, was very easy to turn even with the primitive tools available at the time. Millet flourished in it, as it

▲ The Yangshao Culture produced elegant hand-made pottery, such as this painted red jar, which dates from about 2000 B.C.E. The black and red geometric patterns are characteristic of pottery from the Machang Phase (a clearly distinguished northwestern phase of the Yangshao Culture).

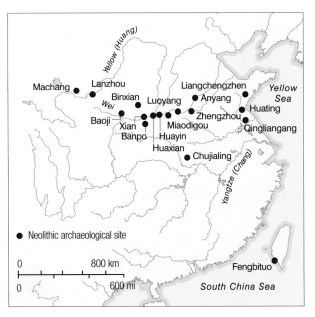

● Neolithic archaeological site

0 ——— 800 km
0 ——— 600 mi

◄ Map of major Chinese Neolithic sites (7000–1500 B.C.E.). From about 7000 B.C.E. onward, settled agricultural communities based on the cultivation of millet spread along the Yellow (Huang) River Valley in the north. A separate, rice-based agriculture developed in the Yangtze (Chang) Valley from about 5000 B.C.E. on.

does to this day, and the early farmers supplemented this staple grain with cabbages, plums, hazelnuts, chestnuts, and hemp (to provide fiber for clothing).

A site at Banpo on the western edge of the Yellow (Huang) River country gives a picture of the lives of the early farmers. Some 600 people lived there in huts whose walls were made from wattle and daub. The roofs were covered with mud-plastered twigs and reeds. Most had floors of compacted earth sunk below ground level. A hearth in the center of each house provided warmth and fire for cooking.

The phase of Chinese prehistory to which Banpo belonged is known as the Yangshao Culture, named for the site in Henan province where its remains were first discovered in the 1920s. A common feature of the Yangshao sites, which are clustered in the Yellow (Huang) River area, are elegant painted pots and bowls made without the aid of the potter's wheel.

Besides raising millet, the Yangshao villagers kept domesticated dogs and pigs and hunted wild game. The cocoons of silkworm moths found in some settlements suggest that they had already mastered basic methods of silk-making.

A different kind of agriculture developed in the Yangtze (Chang) Valley farther south. Wild rice was first domesticated there in about 5000 B.C.E., with the help of artificial pools known as paddies that kept the plant's roots under water. The rice growers lived in solid timber houses, some raised on wooden stilts in the wetlands of the Yangtze Delta.

The move to urban living

Chinese culture moved into a new, urban phase in the Longshan period from about 2500 B.C.E. By this time goats, sheep, cattle, and chickens had been domesticated and the potter's wheel introduced.

People traveled farther afield, and increased contact between communities created opportunities for trade but also for war—Longshan settlements were fortified, surrounded by high earthen walls.

The inhabitants of the towns had learned how to work metals, and they used their skills to make weapons, particularly bows and arrows. While in the early villages all people had equal status, the citizens of the new towns were divided between rich and poor. Some went to their graves surrounded by finely crafted grave goods, others with nothing at all. Chinese society had become more advanced, but also more violent and divided.

▼ The patterns on Yangshao pottery are thought to have developed from realistic depictions (such as a fish) to abstract geometric designs.

▼ A Chinese Neolithic village. The houses had floors of beaten earth and walls made of wattle and daub. The large conical roofs with overhanging eaves were supported by wooden posts inside. The men of the village spent their time fishing and hunting, while the women looked after the home.

11

The Roots of Chinese History

THE CHINESE WERE PIONEERS OF written history—more than two millennia ago they were already compiling detailed accounts of their past. The greatest of the early chroniclers was Sima Qian, official historian to a Han emperor at the end of the second century B.C.E. Even at that time he had a wealth of documents to draw on, and he gave a detailed overview of China's past in his *Historical Records*.

A distinctive feature of the early histories was that they incorporated all the available material about the past, including legend alongside known fact. The version of China's early history that they pieced together was passed down over the centuries and became deeply embedded in the nation's mindset.

Legendary heroes

The story began in pure myth with a sequence of superhuman emperors who were accorded impossibly long life spans. They were succeeded by Fu Xi, a legendary being, both man and woman, who supposedly gave birth to the human race. Fu Xi was the first of a series of culture heroes—familiar figures in mythologies around the world that are used to explain the first appearance of essential skills. So Fu Xi was credited with mastering fire and making the first nets for hunting and fishing.

Fu Xi was the first of a trio of culture heroes known as the Three Sovereigns. His successor, Shen Nong, introduced agriculture, and so can be linked with the Yangshao Culture, the period in which farming villages developed. He also introduced

▲ According to tradition, the legendary emperor Fu Xi ruled for more than 100 years. He is usually depicted as having a dragon-shaped body with a human face, and was said to be the inventor of fire, fishing, and trapping.

▼ Among his other skills, Fu Xi is said to have devised the eight trigrams, a collection of ancient symbols that form the basis of Chinese writing.

the Five Grains on which early Chinese farmers depended. They were barley, two types of millet, hemp, and pulses.

Next came Huang Di, the Yellow Emperor, the legendary ancestor of the Chinese people. Supposedly born in 2704 B.C.E., he was given credit for developing all the arts of civilization, introducing mathematical calculations and the calendar, inventing boats and wagons, bringing money into use, and organizing the first religious ceremonies. Later Chinese saw him as an important father figure under whom civilized life and imperial order first flourished.

The Sage Kings

Some 400 years after the age of the Three Sovereigns came the era of the Sage Kings. Again they formed a trio—Yao, Shun, and Yu—who between them were thought to have ruled from about 2300 to 2100 B.C.E. Although still legendary, they were fully human figures with no supernatural features. Some of their supposed deeds undoubtedly had their counterparts in real life.

Yao was revered in later times as the model ruler, praised by the philosopher Confucius as the greatest of kings. Although famines and floods constantly afflicted his realm, he worked tirelessly for the well-being of his subjects. He was succeeded by the humbly born Shun, a simple farmer whom Yao personally selected as his heir. Shun introduced standardized weights and measures and divided China up into provinces.

Shun's successor Yu went down in the chronicles first and foremost as a flood-tamer who fought long and hard to keep China's rivers within their banks. The Yellow (Huang) River, around which China's early civilization developed, was notorious for disastrous floods that over the centuries cost millions of lives. Stories of Yu's attempts to build dikes and construct drainage channels almost certainly echoed real-life projects to control water in early China.

Unlike Yao and Shun, Yu reportedly passed the throne to his son, thereby starting the first dynasty, the Xia. Although clear archaeological proof has yet to be found, historians now think it likely that some such early state did exist in the Longshan period of China's prehistory, probably somewhere along the middle reaches of the Yellow (Huang) River. With the Xia Dynasty, legend finally merges into reality, and history takes over from myth in the unwinding scroll recording China's past (see map on page 17).

◀ Four miles (6 km) southwest of Shaoxing In eastern China stands an ancient temple. It was built to commemorate the mythical emperor Yu ("Yu the Great"), founder of the Xia Dynasty.

The Shang Dynasty

A HUNDRED YEARS AGO SCHOLARS thought that the Shang Dynasty, like its predecessor the Xia, belonged to legend rather than history. What changed their minds was an extraordinary piece of historical detective work. Over a period of decades, farmers dug up more than 100,000 "oracle bones" near Anyang in north central China—according to tradition the Shang kings' last capital. Initially ground up and sold by quack doctors as "dragons' bones," they were later found to bear inscriptions made by diviners in answer to questions placed by the Shang kings. By studying the inscriptions, researchers were able to draw up a king list that closely matched one written by the historian Sima Qian more than 2,000 years ago.

The traditional accounts claimed that the first Shang king seized power from the last ruler of the Xia Dynasty in 1766 B.C.E. The area that he and his successors ruled may have covered up to 40,000 square miles (100,000 sq. km) of the Yellow (Huang) River Valley's middle reaches. They called it the Middle Kingdom, because less developed states surrounded it on all sides. The name stuck, and later dynasties would use it to describe China as a beacon of civilization in a backward world (see map on page 17).

Social hierarchy and organization

The Shang monarchs ruled a Bronze Age kingdom in which an elite of aristocratic warriors, equipped with chariots and bronze weapons, ruled over a peasantry who had only tools of stone, bone, and wood. The nobles lived in substantial houses set in walled compounds. Their chief pleasure was hunting.

At the top of the social pyramid was the king. He was a religious as well as a political leader and was called the Son of Heaven. He alone could mediate with the supreme Shang deity, believed to be his own divine ancestor ruling over heaven.

In theory the king was a godlike figure who owned all the lands in his realm, but in practice he ruled in consultation with a council of leading nobles. The aristocracy also provided the monarch with officers to lead the royal armies in time of war. The troops were organized in companies of 100 men armed with bows, lances, and battle axes, complemented by squadrons of chariots manned by archers and lancers. Battles were fought to a musical accompaniment of drums and bells.

▲ The rulers of the Shang Dynasty were very superstitious. They asked their court diviners to predict many things: the weather, health, farming, and fortune. The questions and answers were carved on animal bones, known as "oracle bones."

The fate of defeated soldiers was grim, since the Shang carried out human and animal sacrifice on a large scale, and prisoners of war were often the victims of this practice. Priests offered up sacrifices to please gods as well as to ensure good harvests or successful military campaigns. They also killed large numbers of human victims to accompany dead rulers to the grave. Excavations of royal tombs at Anyang have turned up hundreds of skeletons—some decapitated, others with hands tied behind their backs. Dead sentries and guard dogs protected the tomb chamber itself, while rows of chariots, complete with executed horses and charioteers, lined the path.

The tombs also contained magnificent grave goods that show Shang civilization in a more positive light. Trade flourished in the towns that grew up at the time, and craftsmen produced

▶ In this drawing of a hunting expedition, the king stands on the left-hand side of the chariot, his attendant on the right, and the charioteer at the front. The chariot was made of wood, with bronze fittings.

Shang Rulers
c.1766–1300 B.C.E. A series of kings, beginning with Tang and ending with Yang Jia
1300–1251 B.C.E. Pan Geng, Xiao Xin, and Xiao Yi
1250–1192 Wu Ding
1191–1148 Zu Geng, Zu Jia, Lin Xin, and Kang Ding
1147–1113 Wu Yi
1112–1102 Wen Ding
1101–1076 Di Yi
1075–1046 Di Xin

splendid works in bronze and jade. The art of writing was also well developed by now, as the inscriptions on the oracle bones demonstrate.

A succession of 30 kings ruled the Shang kingdom for some 600 years, until the 12th or 11th century B.C.E. Then, according to the histories, an oppressive and corrupt monarch named Di Xin lost the support of his subjects. The ruler of a neighboring realm, that of the Zhou people living to the west of the Shang, led the resistance to the tyrant. After being defeated in battle, Di Xin retreated to his capital and killed himself. Power in China passed to new Zhou masters.

▶ A Chinese archaeologist works at one of seven pits unearthed in 2005 in the ruins of Yin, near Anyang city in north-central China. Five of the seven newly discovered pits are arranged in a line, with chariots and horses all facing eastward.

The Zhou Dynasty

THE ZHOU DYNASTY TOOK OVER FROM THE Shang. The new king rewarded his family and followers with large fiefs (areas of land) carved from the lands of the conquered aristocracy. But for most of the population life continued much as before. If anything, the feudal system became more deeply entrenched. Vassal lords "paid" for their fiefs in tribute and military service. With the help of these aristocrats, the early kings extended the borders of their realm—at their widest they reached south to the Yangtze (Chang) River and east to the Yellow Sea.

Tension remained high on the realm's northern and eastern frontiers, where the Zhou fought a series of border wars with nomadic tribes. During the reign of the 12th king, the tribes finally succeeded in breaking through, aided by a rebel faction at court. In 771 B.C.E.—events can be dated accurately from that time on—the invaders sacked the Zhou capital, Hao, forcing subsequent kings to rule from Luoyang, located farther from the frontier. Historians label the years after the move the Eastern Zhou period.

Traditionally, the Eastern Zhou years themselves have been divided into two parts. The earlier (771 to 481 B.C.E.) is known as the Spring and Autumn (Fall) period, because its main events were recorded in China's most ancient historical chronicle, the *Spring and Autumn Annals*. This was a time of crucial change. The monarchy's authority had been fatally weakened by the events of 771. Power devolved to great feudal lords ruling over what amounted to separate states, paying little more than lip service to their Zhou overlords in Luoyang. These multiple petty kingdoms existed in a state of rivalry that always threatened to boil over into open war.

The age of technology

Important developments were also under way in society at large. Iron was widely available from the seventh century B.C.E. The use of metal plows and other implements vastly increased agricultural productivity, spurring a population growth that encouraged the expansion of towns and trade. A merchant class developed, although its members were despised. The feudal system fell into disarray as Chinese society became more complex and dynamic.

The innovations introduced in the Spring and Autumn period became more pronounced and more lethal in the succeeding Warring States era (481 to 221 B.C.E.). By that time the number of rival states had shrunk dramatically as a result of conquest and annexation. Eventually only seven major kingdoms remained, locked in perpetual conflict.

The nature of warfare had changed, too. Metal weapons had become widely available, and the days when chariot-borne warriors could sweep away all before them were gone. With the invention of the crossbow in the fourth century B.C.E., peasant archers had the means to kill even heavily armored noblemen from a distance.

Zhou Rulers			
1046–1043	Wuwang	612–607	Kuangwang
1042–1021	Chengwang	606–586	Dingwang
1020–996	Kangwang	585–572	Jianwang
995–977	Zhaowang	571–545	Lingwang
976–922	Muwang	544–521	Jingwang
922–900	Gongwang	520	Daiwang
899–892	Yiwang	519–476	Jingwang
891–886	Xiaoawang	475–469	Yuanwang
885–878	Yiwang	468–442	Zhendingwang
877–841	Liwang	441	Aiwang and Siwang
841–828	Gonghe	440–426	Kaowang
827–782	Xuanwang	425–402	Weiliewang
782–770	Youwang	401–376	Anwang
770–720	Pingwang	375–369	Liewang
719–697	Huanwang	368–321	Xianwang
696–682	Zhuangwang	320–315	Shenjingwang
681–677	Xiwang	314–256	Nanwang
676–652	Huiwang	255–249	Huiwang
651–619	Xiangwang		
618–613	Qingwang	(all dates B.C.E.)	

▲ A representation of a Zhou general, based on excavated material. His boots would have been made of leather with metal studs. The bronze breastplate is decorated with a *taotie* monster mask, showing ferocity and strength.

▼ ▶ Advances in metal production paved the way for the development of more effective weapons. The crossbow (right) was the rifle of its day, a lightweight weapon capable of firing accurately and repeatedly over a long range. Below is a model from the Warring States era—its trigger looks very much like that of a modern rifle.

Inner Mongolian
Plateau

*Tengger
Desert*

*Ordos
Desert*

HELAN MOUNTAINS

BAIYU MTS.

LIUPAN MTS.

MIN MOUNTAINS

Baode

Suide

Shilou

Fengxiang
Qin

Baoji

Qishan
Feng
Fufeng

Lintong
Xianyang
Huaxian

Hao

Lantian

**Erlitou
(Zhenling)**

**QIN
MOUNTAINS**

Xiasi

Nanyang

Han

Yangtze

Sanxingdui
Zhuwajie
Juliandun
ngxian
Baimasi

*Sichuan
Basin*

Dongsunba

DALOU MOUNTAINS

Beixinbao

Dongshankou/
Songyuan
Huangtupocun
Liyu

Baoding
Quyang

Pingshan

Xiadu

Yanxiadu
Taixicun

Gaocheng

Sanggan

*Yellow (Huang)
before 602
B.C.E.*

Taiyun

Qixian

Xingtai

Hongtong
Xiangfen
Houma

Yicheng

Anyi
Shan

Jiang
Luoning

Luoyang

Huixian

Xiang

Wu'an
Handan

Anyang

Chaoge
Cao

Zhengzhou

Linru

Xinzheng
Xuchang

Yanling

Yangchen

Xincai

Changtaiguan

Leigudun

Jingshan

Han
Shuihudi

Panlongcheng

Huangpi

Qichun

Ying
Jiangling

Chongyang

Duchang
Wucheng
Xinjian

Ningxiang

Liuchenggiao/
Zoujiatang

Xingan

Machanggou
Nincheng
Lingyuan

Luan

Pinggu
Lijiacun

*Liaodong
Peninsula*

Bo Hai

*Shandong
Peninsula*

Shangwangzhuang
Jinan
Linzi
Sufutun
Yidi

Pingyin
Feicheng
Zhang

Qufu
Zouxian
Tengxian

Liujiadianzi

Lingshanwei

Yellow Sea

Tancheng

Fenghuangling

Xuzhou

Shangqiu
Huaiyang

Chen

Huai

Pingliangtai

Funan

Ximen/
Zhujiaji
Poshankou

Jiashan
Dantu

Feixi

Fenghuangzui/
Jiulidun

Tunxi

Grand Canal

Yangtze (Chang)

Zhuji

Changshu
Gusu

Fenghuangshan/
Xishishan

WUYI MOUNTAINS

*East China
Sea*

*Yellow (Huang)
after 602 B.C.E.*

Grand Canal

Kingdom of tigers and wolves

In those troubled times, the path to supreme power lay open for the state with the largest armies and the most ruthless policies. That dubious honor went to Qin (see pages 20–21). Located in the far west, Qin was seen by people in the Chinese heartland as at best semicivilized—a "kingdom of tigers and wolves."

But its troops were honed by constant strife with the western nomads, and in the third and second centuries B.C.E. it developed a tough ideology that sacrificed all citizens' rights to the demands of military victory. Under a young ruler, Zheng, Qin used its unequaled might to conquer the remaining independent kingdoms one by one. The last, Qi, fell in 221, and Zheng was able to take power over a united China as the First Emperor, Qin Shi Huangdi.

▲ Map showing the known extent of Chinese influence during the Xia, Shang, and Zhou Dynasties. It is based on archaeologists' studies of bronze inscriptions found in numerous sites in the Yellow (Huang) River region of northern China, as well as on later histories.

■ Shang site with rich burial
□ Shang site with finds of oracle bones
△ other major Shang site
■ Zhou cemetery or burial site
□ Zhou bronze hoard
△ other Zhou site
□ other Bronze Age site
⁙ source of copper
⁘ source of tin
━━ core area of Xia Dynasty
━━ maximum extents of Shang Dynasty
▨ Zhou heartland (Zhouyuan)
▨ maximum extents of Zhou Dynasty
▨ extent of Chinese cultural influence, 5th century B.C.E.
┄ ancient course of Yellow (Huang) River
▨ ancient coastline

0   200 km
0   150 mi

The Growth of Cities

SINCE EARLY TIMES THE CHINESE HAVE BEEN an urban people. The first towns grew up in the loess country of the Yellow (Huang) River Valley in the third millennium B.C.E. The development of towns was made possible by the high fertility of the region, which provided food surpluses that could feed a population that did not work the land.

The spread of towns had important social consequences. Archaeological excavations show that, unlike the egalitarianism (equality) of early village life, there were marked differences in wealth among individuals who lived in towns. Many citizens at Chengziyai in Shandong province were laid to rest without coffins in bare earthen pits, but others were buried in caskets surrounded by expensive jade ornaments. The birth of cities and the spread of social rank and classes were intimately intertwined.

One reason for the growth of cities was defense. In the flat lands of northern China the walled town was a place where people could take refuge from danger. In Chinese writing, the pictogram for "city" shows a walled enclosure, and huge efforts went into constructing the fortifications that protected major settlements. Excavations have shown that the city wall at Ao, an early Shang capital near Zhengzhou, was up to 120 feet (36 m) wide at its base, and one estimate suggests that 10,000 laborers would have had to work for 18 years to build it.

▶ Early Chinese cities, such as the ancient city of Pingyao, built during the Zhou Dynasty, were strongly fortified. Steep walls surround Pingyao, stretching for about 4 miles (6 km). The city was also protected by a 10-foot- (3-m-) deep moat.

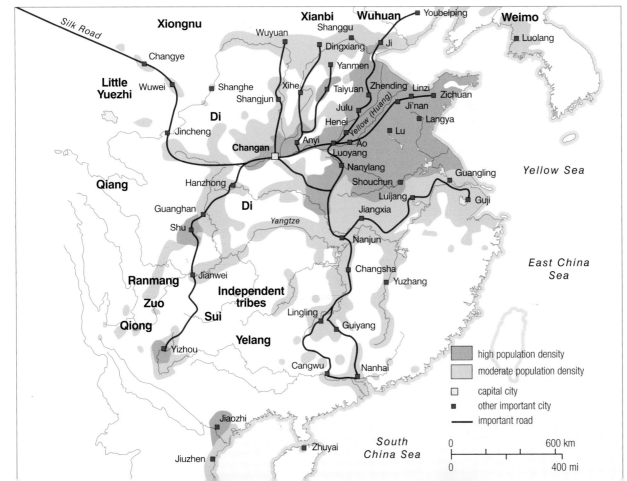

◀ Map showing the distribution of the Chinese population under the Western (Former) Han. The greatest concentration was in the north China plain. Elsewhere, the ethnic Han Chinese population was distributed mostly along the river valleys. The higher ground was left mainly to non-Han peoples. The map reflects the distribution of officially registered citizens only.

Administrative centers

Towns gained fresh importance in the Han period as seats of local government. From early times they had been home to the state granaries where peasants delivered a portion of their crops instead of taxes. Now they also became places where administrators were based and records were stored.

In later eras cities served as barometers for the economic state of the nation. They generally thrived in the climate of political stability provided by the great dynasties. In Tang times the nation's capital, Changan, had an estimated 2 million inhabitants. The city was laid out on a grid scheme with some avenues as much as 500 feet (150 m) wide. It had a central palace area, an entertainment district, two main street markets, and 109 demarcated neighborhoods. Under the Song, almost 15 percent of the total population lived in cities with 100,000 or more inhabitants, at a time when many of the West's largest capitals numbered only tens of thousands.

The tradition of urban living established under the first dynasties proved to be an enduring feature of Chinese life. It lasted through all the various changes of regime that affected the country over the next four millennia, and it survives to this day— in 2006 the nation had 34 agglomerations that had more than 1 million inhabitants, and the urban population totaled 465 million people.

In the troubled times of the later Zhou period, urban centers grew up around the fortified strongholds of the nobility. An enthusiasm for town planning also developed. Yanxiadu, the capital of the northeastern state of Yan, was subdivided by earthen walls into three distinct sections: industrial, commercial, and residential. Barracks were built close to the gates to house sentries who kept an eye on everyone entering or leaving the city.

By that time people were flocking to the towns. One observer wrote of Linzi, capital of the state of Qi, that "its streets are so crammed that the carriages rub rims, and its populace so great that the people rub shoulders." This trait became even more marked in the succeeding Han era, by which time China had an estimated 6 million city dwellers. They were attracted by the economic opportunities that they found in the crowded streets. It was said that an artisan or trader could earn enough money in 24 hours to live on for five days, whereas a peasant farmer might labor all year long and still not be able to feed himself.

▶ With the spread of urban living, a desire for town planning developed. Shown here is a plan of the city and palace of Xingqing, built at Changan (near present-day Xian) in 714 C.E.

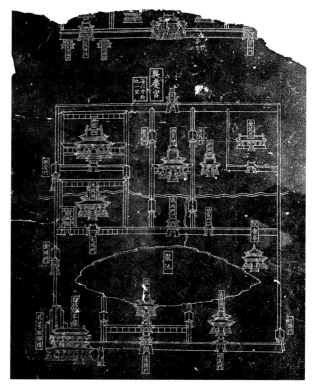

The Qin Empire

Urumqi Qit
Kashgar Kucha Karashahr Turfan
Wu Lei
Yarkand Ying-pan
Takla Makan Desert
Loulan
Khotan Cherchen
KARAKORUM MOUNTAINS Niya ALTUN MOUNTAINS
KUNLUN SHAN

THE QIN EMPIRE LASTED BARELY 14 YEARS, yet it transformed China. It was set up in 221 B.C.E. when the state of Qin finally succeeded in crushing the last of the Warring States, uniting China for the first time in centuries. The Qin king then changed his title to Shi Huangdi, the First Emperor.

Aided by his chief minister Li Su, Shi Huangdi began a program of changes that effectively destroyed the nation's old feudal order. The ruling classes of the conquered states lost their estates and were forced to take up residence in the Qin capital of Xianyang under the watchful eye of the emperor himself. Huge quantities of weapons were destroyed and melted down to make statues. To undermine the control of the land that had given the nobility their power, peasant farmers were given the right to own, buy, and sell the fields they worked. No longer were they the vassals of aristocratic landowners—instead, they became tax-paying subjects of the emperor.

One nation divided and united

The feudal nobility also lost their role as governors and administrators. China's many kingdoms were abolished, and the nation was partitioned into 36 provinces that were themselves subdivided into smaller administrative units all the way down to village level. Each province was governed by an official appointed by and answerable to the emperor.

The First Emperor and his ministers set about uniting their vast realm in other ways. They introduced a single currency across the nation and imposed a uniform system of weights and measures. Axle lengths were standardized so that all across China carts could trundle in the same ruts. Most important of all, the entire nation was forced to use the Chinese characters employed in the state of Qin, thereby unifying the written language. It is largely thanks to this reform that all Chinese people speak and read one language today, rather than dozens of regional dialects.

Having brought peace to the nation, Shi Huangdi used forced labor to undertake public works projects on a massive scale. He linked a series of existing defensive walls that kept northern nomads from China's agricultural lands to create the first version of the Great Wall of China, 1,400 miles (2,250 km) long (see pages 76–77). He constructed the Magic Transport Canal linking two rivers in the Yangtze (Chang) Valley—opening 1,250 miles (2,000 km) of inland waterway to barge navigation. New roads radiated out of Xianyang, connecting the Qin capital to the rest of the kingdom.

To enforce unity, the First Emperor also cracked down on dissent. When Confucian scholars

▶ In Qin times the cavalry uniform was well designed for mounted warfare. Cavalrymen wore relatively close-fitting tunics and large shin guards over leather boots. The horses' harnesses were made of leather straps and bronze rings and knobs.

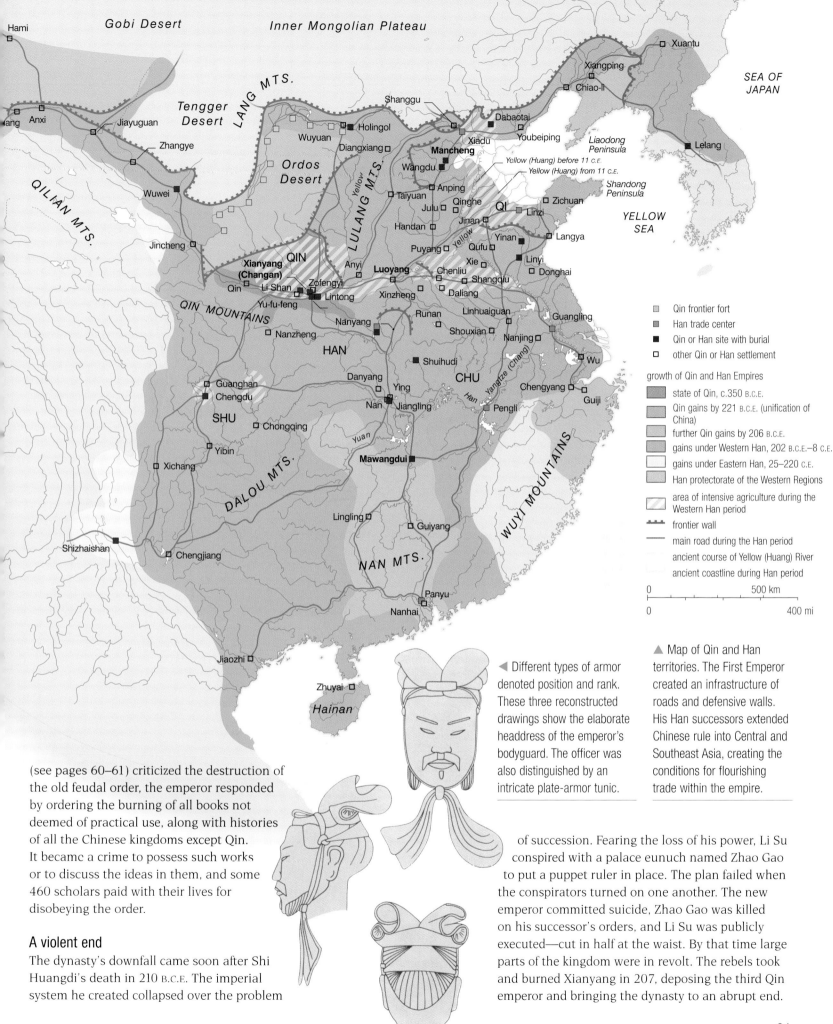

Hami

Gobi Desert　　　*Inner Mongolian Plateau*

Xuantu

Xiangping

Chiao-li

SEA OF
JAPAN

ang　Anxi

Jiayuguan

LANG MTS.

Tengger
Desert

Shanggu

Dabaotai

Xiadu

Youbeiping

*Liaodong
Peninsula*

Lelang

Holingol

Wuyuan

Wangdu

Mancheng

Yellow (Huang) before 11 C.E.
Yellow (Huang) from 11 C.E.

Diangxiang

Xiangping

Wuwei

Zhangye

QILIAN MTS.

Ordos
Desert

Yellow MTS.

LULANG MTS.

Taiyuan

Anping

*Shandong
Peninsula*

YELLOW
SEA

Jincheng

QIN

**Xianyang
(Changan)**

Qin

Li Shan

Yu-fu-feng

QIN MOUNTAINS

Zofengyi

Lintong

Anyi

Luoyang

Qinghe

Julu

Jinan

QI

Zichuan

Linzi

Langya

Qufu

Yinan

Xie

Linyi

Donghai

Handan

Puyang

Chenliu

Shangqiu

Xinzheng

Daliang

Nanyang

Nanzheng

HAN

Runan

Linhuaiguan

Shouxian

Nanjing

Guangling

Wu

Shuihudi

CHU

Chengyang

Guiji

Danyang

Ying

Yangtze (Chang)

Pengli

Guanghan

Chengdu

SHU

Jiangling

Han

Yuan

Chongqing

Nan

Yibin

Xichang

DALOU MTS.

Mawangdui

WUYI MOUNTAINS

Lingling

Guiyang

Shizhaishan

Chengjiang

NAN MTS.

Panyu

Nanhai

Zhuyai

Hainan

Jiaozhi

□ Qin frontier fort
■ Han trade center
■ Qin or Han site with burial
□ other Qin or Han settlement

growth of Qin and Han Empires

state of Qin, c.350 B.C.E.
Qin gains by 221 B.C.E. (unification of China)
further Qin gains by 206 B.C.E.
gains under Western Han, 202 B.C.E.–8 C.E.
gains under Eastern Han, 25–220 C.E.
Han protectorate of the Western Regions
area of intensive agriculture during the Western Han period
frontier wall
main road during the Han period
ancient course of Yellow (Huang) River
ancient coastline during Han period

0　　　　　500 km
0　　　　　400 mi

◀ Different types of armor
denoted position and rank.
These three reconstructed
drawings show the elaborate
headdress of the emperor's
bodyguard. The officer was
also distinguished by an
intricate plate-armor tunic.

▲ Map of Qin and Han
territories. The First Emperor
created an infrastructure of
roads and defensive walls.
His Han successors extended
Chinese rule into Central and
Southeast Asia, creating the
conditions for flourishing
trade within the empire.

(see pages 60–61) criticized the destruction of
the old feudal order, the emperor responded
by ordering the burning of all books not
deemed of practical use, along with histories
of all the Chinese kingdoms except Qin.
It became a crime to possess such works
or to discuss the ideas in them, and some
460 scholars paid with their lives for
disobeying the order.

A violent end
The dynasty's downfall came soon after Shi
Huangdi's death in 210 B.C.E. The imperial
system he created collapsed over the problem

of succession. Fearing the loss of his power, Li Su
conspired with a palace eunuch named Zhao Gao
to put a puppet ruler in place. The plan failed when
the conspirators turned on one another. The new
emperor committed suicide, Zhao Gao was killed
on his successor's orders, and Li Su was publicly
executed—cut in half at the waist. By that time large
parts of the kingdom were in revolt. The rebels took
and burned Xianyang in 207, deposing the third Qin
emperor and bringing the dynasty to an abrupt end.

The Han Dynasty

LASTING FOR MORE THAN 400 YEARS (WITH a brief interruption), the Han Dynasty was one of the most enduring in China's history. It emerged from the ruins of the short-lived Qin Empire when a commoner named Liu Bang took advantage of the prevailing chaos to seize power. He named the dynasty he founded after the kingdom of Han, which he had ruled briefly during his rise to the throne.

Twelve emperors followed Liu Bang until Wang Mang, an imperial regent, declared himself emperor in 9 C.E., establishing the Xin ("New") Dynasty. He was overthrown 14 years later, and by 25 C.E. the Han were back in power. The original capital of Changan was burned in the fighting, so the new emperor moved his headquarters 250 miles (400 km) east to Luoyang. The era following the Xin is therefore known as the Eastern (or Latter) Han period, in contrast to the earlier Western (or Former) Han time.

The Han era was an age of cultural achievement. Scholars took part in affairs of state, and there was no more burning of books (see pages 20–21). Confucianism became the ruling ideology, and it was formally proclaimed as such in 136 B.C.E. (see pages 60–61). One Eastern Han emperor even had a definitive edition of the Confucian classics engraved in stone.

The Han Empire

The Han rulers established an efficient, unified administration (see pages 24–25). They set taxes based on nationwide censuses of population and

▶ The 12th-century Chinese painter Zhao Boju painted large landscapes portraying historical events. Here, a section from *The First Emperor of the Han Dynasty Entering Kuan Tung* shows a detail of the royal entourage in the mountains.

▼ Han Dynasty rubbings of figures from battle scenes, taken from the Wu family tombs at Shandong. They show the style of dress and armor of the time.

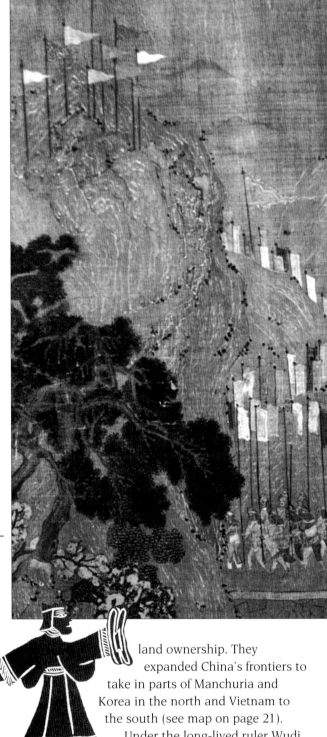

Han Rulers

Western Han	Eastern Han
206–195 B.C.E. Gaodi (Liu Bang)	**25–57 C.E.** Guangwudi
	57–75 C.E. Mingdi
195 B.C.E.–9 C.E. 12 emperors: Huidi, Shaodi Kong, Wendi, Jingdi, Wudi, Zhaodi, Xuandi, Yuandi, Chengdi, Aidi, Pingdi, and Ruzi	**75–88 C.E.** Zhangdi
	88–106 C.E. Hedi
	106 C.E. Shangdi
	106–125 C.E. Andi
	125–144 C.E. Shundi
Xin	**144–145 C.E.** Chongdi
9–23 C.E. Wang Mang	**145–146 C.E.** Zhidi
23–25 C.E. Huaiyang Wang	**146–168 C.E.** Huandi
	168–189 C.E. Lingdi
	189–220 C.E. Xiandi

land ownership. They expanded China's frontiers to take in parts of Manchuria and Korea in the north and Vietnam to the south (see map on page 21).

Under the long-lived ruler Wudi (the name means Martial Emperor), they fought an epic series of wars with the Xiongnu nomads north of the Great Wall, the people known in the West as the Huns. The military effort held the steppe horsemen back but failed to conquer them, and the cost of the campaigns exhausted the Han treasury.

Infighting and corruption

Factionalism and intrigue were recurrent problems. The emperors had many consorts (partners), and the principal wives all wanted their own children to inherit the throne. Under weak emperors an inner circle of palace attendants, many of them eunuchs, gained an unhealthy influence over state affairs. To compound the problem, no fewer than eight of the 12 emperors of the Latter Han period came to the throne as minors below the age of 15.

Matters came to a head under Lingdi, who reigned for 21 years from 168 C.E. Corruption reached a peak as court officials openly sold the highest positions in the land. Peasant unrest broke out into open revolt under the leadership of revolutionaries known as the Yellow Turbans.

Following the emperor's death in 189, the military invaded the palace, massacring more than 2,000 eunuchs, but by then the damage was done. Over the next three decades the nation fell apart as rival warlords vied for power. When the last Han emperor finally stepped down in the year 220, China's unity was a thing of the past, and more than 350 years would pass before the nation came together again.

Throughout the Han period rulers struggled to pay their way, largely because they could not raise enough money from taxes. Too much money was concentrated in the hands of wealthy landowners, who paid relatively little in taxes, while the peasantry, who could barely make ends meet, paid more. To remedy this imbalance, Wang Mang sought to nationalize the land and redistribute it to the people who worked it. He was brought down, however, by a combination of natural disaster—severe flooding changed the course of the Yellow (Huang) River in his reign—and vested interests, and his reform program largely died with him.

▶ This ceramic sculpture in the form of a mounted archer dates from the Han Dynasty and was probably made between 50 B.C.E. and 50 C.E.

An Administrative Empire

ON PAPER AT LEAST, THE ADMINISTRATIVE system that Han rulers borrowed from the First Emperor of the Qin (see pages 20–21) was well designed. It took the form of a pyramid whose base was made up of village councils. Above the villages were communes and districts, then county-sized prefectures that in turn were grouped into "commanderies" the size of small states. Many had, in fact, been just that in the earlier Warring States period, but under the Han they were safely embraced within the imperial scheme.

Top of the pyramid of power

At the apex of the hierarchy of civil servants staffing the pyramid was the emperor himself, who made the principal appointments and supervised the entire system. Three advisers, or exellencies, helped him: a chancellor in charge of state finances, an imperial counsellor who headed the imperial bureaucracy, and the commander-in-chief of the army.

Below them were the officials in charge of the principal ministries, with responsibility for such matters as palace security, foreign affairs, and criminal prosecutions. One had joint care of religious rituals, astronomical observations, and record-keeping. There were also lesser offices. One that attained considerable influence under the long-lived emperor Wudi was the Bureau of Music, whose staff collected folk songs, maintained choirs and orchestras, and provided performances for official occasions.

In practice the governmental apparatus was never quite as neat in its working as its designers might have wished. In reaction against the Qin Dynasty's suppression of local rule, separate kingdoms reasserted themselves in early Han times. Although Liu Bang, the dynasty's founder, took care to place these statelets in the hands of relatives and supporters who were willing to acknowledge his overlordship, their very existence helped rekindle the flames of separatism. Liu Bang himself was killed while trying to bring one to heel. Later emperors reduced the kingdoms' independence until they had little more autonomy than the commanderies, whose own number grew as the empire expanded—by late Han times there were 83.

One of the great achievements of the Han rulers was the creation of a dedicated and efficient civil service, staffed for the most part by the best available talents (see pages 22–23). Under Wudi, top officials were instructed to select suitable candidates from the provinces, who were then sent to the capital for training. Those who did well were put on a year's probation, and were subsequently subjected to performance reviews every three years.

Although a full-scale system of formal exams was not introduced until Tang times (see pages 32–33), future administrators were already quizzed on their knowledge and opinions, and the emperor himself is said to have taken a keen interest in the views they expressed. The model administrator was said to be a man distinguished by respect for the family, loyalty to the emperor, moral rectitude, and deep learning—qualities that characterized the doctrine of Confucius (see pages 60–61).

Rewards of high office

Those who graduated to posts in the central government or in provincial administration could count on rewards that included job security and substantial privileges. They were exempted from army conscription and forced-labor duties, and given one day off work in every five. In addition, they could look forward to regular promotions if they performed well. There were 12 grades from the lowest to the highest posts, with the uppermost administrators receiving 20 times the salary of the lowest rank, paid partly in grain and partly in cash.

Yet the Han system was not without flaws. There was favoritism in the selection process—nothing kept the officials who ran it from nominating their own or their friends' sons for these appointments. A far deeper problem lay at the top of the hierarchy, with the rise to power of an inner court of imperial attendants, mostly palace eunuchs. They could use their privileged access to the emperor to bypass and subvert the official system. Yet under strong rulers the Han bureaucracy in China probably gave better service than any the world had yet seen. It provided a model administrative system that was to help hold the nation together for the next 2,000 years.

▶ Far right. Structure of the Han administrative system. The emperor oversaw the running of state affairs, aided by three main advisers. Based on the hierarchy established under the Qin, it was to form a lasting model for government in China.

▶ Under the Han, government officials were important figures, respected for their education and rewarded well for their service. These pottery figures represent officials from a later period—their prominence in society dates back to the Han.

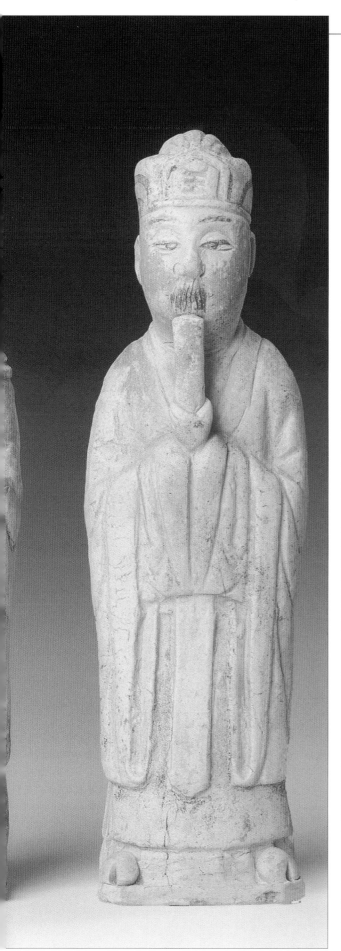

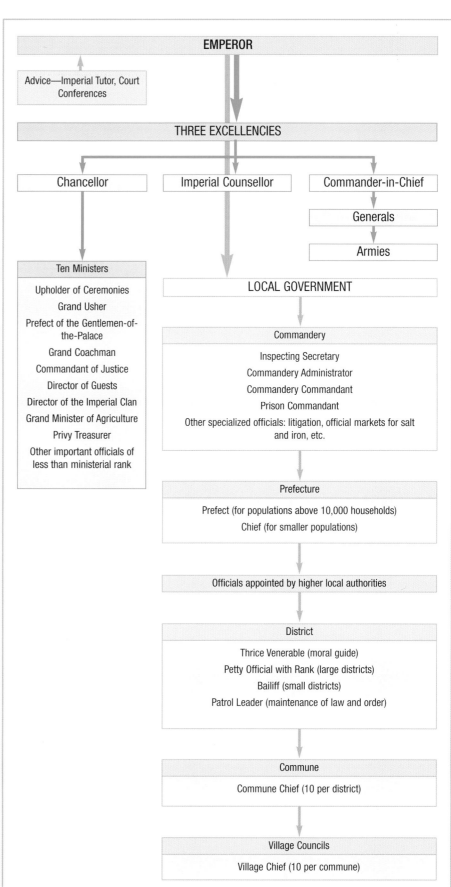

EMPEROR

Advice—Imperial Tutor, Court Conferences

THREE EXCELLENCIES

| Chancellor | Imperial Counsellor | Commander-in-Chief |

Generals

Armies

Ten Ministers

Upholder of Ceremonies

Grand Usher

Prefect of the Gentlemen-of-the-Palace

Grand Coachman

Commandant of Justice

Director of Guests

Director of the Imperial Clan

Grand Minister of Agriculture

Privy Treasurer

Other important officials of less than ministerial rank

LOCAL GOVERNMENT

Commandery

Inspecting Secretary

Commandery Administrator

Commandery Commandant

Prison Commandant

Other specialized officials: litigation, official markets for salt and iron, etc.

Prefecture

Prefect (for populations above 10,000 households)

Chief (for smaller populations)

Officials appointed by higher local authorities

District

Thrice Venerable (moral guide)

Petty Official with Rank (large districts)

Bailiff (small districts)

Patrol Leader (maintenance of law and order)

Commune

Commune Chief (10 per district)

Village Councils

Village Chief (10 per commune)

Links With the West

CHINA'S FIRST SIGNIFICANT VENTURE westward was in the second century B.C.E., when the Han emperor Wudi was at war with the Xiongnu Huns. He heard of potential allies called the Yuezhi who lived beyond the Huns' western borders, and he decided to send envoys to contact them. The man who led the expedition, Zhang Qian, was captured, along with the rest of his party, and held prisoner by the Xiongnu for 10 years. Eventually he escaped and found his way to Bactria in Central Asia. Returning through Xiongnu territory, he was again taken into custody, and only arrived back at the Han court in 126 B.C.E., 12 years after he had set out. He was accompanied by a Xiongnu wife and one other survivor of the original party of about 100 men.

Zhang brought back animal and plant specimens, including cultivated grapes and walnuts. He also regaled the court with tales of rich lands whose rulers rode on elephants and of a place called Ferghana (now in Afghanistan), where fine horses could be had in exchange for Chinese silks.

Emergence of the Silk Road

The long-term result of Zhang's venture was the establishment of the Silk Road, a lengthy series of overland trading routes through the deserts of Central Asia and on to Parthia that passed cities such as Samarkand, Ray, and Hecatompylos. There Chinese traders swapped not just silk but also gold, cinnamon, and animal skins for wine, spices, linen, wool, foodstuffs, and horses.

There they also heard tales of a great empire in the west that they called Da Qin—their name for Rome. Fearful of losing their lucrative role as middlemen, the Parthians tried to prevent any direct contact between the two powers. The earliest known

▼ After a long and arduous journey lasting almost four years, Marco Polo reached China in 1275. His arrival is depicted in this undated illustration. Polo's travels were described in the book *Il Milione* by Rustichello of Pisa.

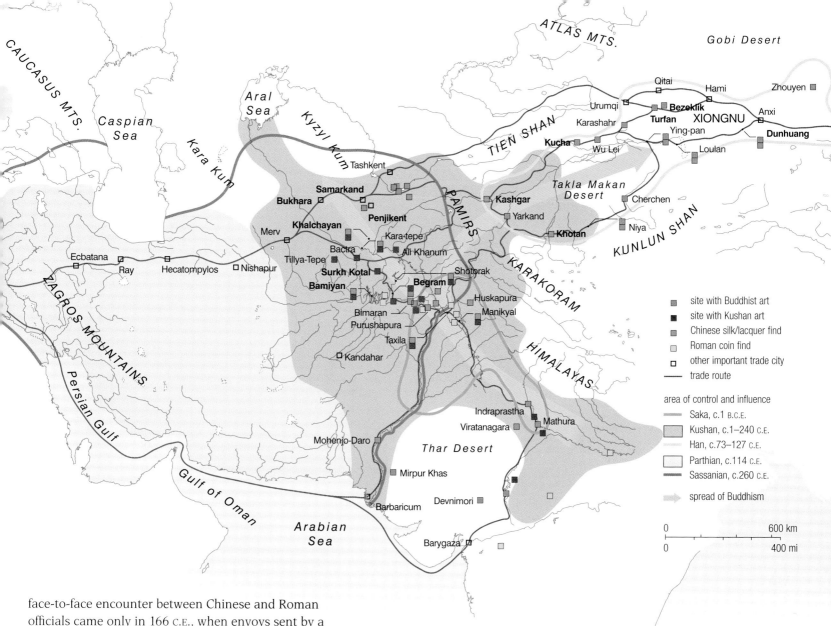

face-to-face encounter between Chinese and Roman officials came only in 166 C.E., when envoys sent by a ruler described in Chinese annals as "Andun, king of Da Qin"—presumably the Roman emperor Marcus Aurelius—arrived in China bringing gifts of ivory, tortoiseshell, and rhinoceros horn.

The Silk Road's importance as a trading artery changed over the centuries. It was particularly busy in Tang times, when a westward drive briefly took Chinese armies to Iran and the borders of the Islamic caliphate. Overland travel between east and west was easiest six centuries later under the rule of the Mongols (see pages 42–43). Although at first they brought devastation, the Mongols later imposed peace across much of Eurasia, from Syria and southern Russia all the way to Korea. It was during their time that the Venetian merchant Marco Polo (1254–1324) was able to journey to Kublai Khan's capital of Dadu (modern Beijing), returning to Italy by way of Sumatra, southern India, and Persia.

Polo returned by boat. It was also on ships that Marcus Aurelius's envoys had reached the Chinese court. The sea route through the Indian Ocean was China's other portal to the west, complementing the Silk Road. China maintained trading relations with

India and Persia at least from Han times, although the goods passed through the hands of a succession of intermediaries in Southeast Asia and the East Indies rather than by direct means.

Exploration by sea

That situation could have changed in 1405, when the Ming emperor Yongle sent Admiral Zheng He on the first of seven remarkable ocean voyages. These expeditions took Chinese ships to the coasts of India, the Persian Gulf, and East Africa, from where they returned bearing giraffes, ostriches, and zebras, among other gifts. If the emperors had chosen to follow up these probes, China could well have come to dominate the southern Asian trade routes. As it turned out, however, there was a change of policy at court after Zheng He's last voyage in 1433, and the government abandoned maritime expansion. China turned in on itself, and the way was left open instead for European merchants to trade with India and the Spice Islands in the wake of the pioneering voyages of Vasco da Gama and Magellan.

▲ Map of the Silk Road as it traverses the inhospitable region of deserts, mountains, and high plateaus between China and Iran. In reality, the "Road" was a series of ancient routes. Throughout several centuries it was a source of wealth for many cities, kingdoms, and empires. It was also the path for the spread of Buddhism east to China and of Chinese products to the West. Even Roman coins have been found along the route.

The Six Dynasties

THE PERIOD FROM 220 TO 581 IS NAMED FOR six successive dynasties that had their capitals at Jiankang during this time. After the Han Dynasty collapsed in 200, China split into three competing kingdoms ruled by warlords. The northern realm, with about 29 million people, was ruled by the Wei Dynasty. The Wu kingdom in the less crowded south covered a wider area but had only about 11 million subjects, while the western Shu state was the smallest, with fewer than 8 million.

The three were briefly reunited in the late third century by a general, Sima Jian, who seized control of Wei and then conquered the other two states. Yet, in the north of China at least, the Jin Dynasty that he founded did not survive long after his death in 290. His sons fought among each other for succession, and one made the fatal mistake of turning to the Xiongnu nomads, China's traditional enemies, for help. These herders had been allowed to settle inside the Great Wall since late Han times. Now they set up a kingdom of their own. They rapidly conquered all of northern China, causing death and devastation. The Jin capital of Luoyang was sacked in 311; the old Han city of Changan suffered a similar fate in 316.

"Barbarian" invasions

The Xiongnu were not the only non-Chinese ethnic group to take advantage of the chaos in the north. In the fourth century a succession of invaders, such as the Juan-Juan and Xianbi, struggled for power, launching the period known as the 16 Kingdoms of the Five Barbarian Peoples. At one stage a Tibetan

▶ Map of China showing 350 years of disunity. After the fall of the Han Dynasty in 220, China split into three separate kingdoms: the Wei in the north (which included the wealthy Yellow [Huang] River Valley), the Wu in the south, and the Shu to the west. After a lengthy period of disunity and invasions from the north, the nation was finally reunited in 589 at the start of the Sui Dynasty.

▼ Painted pottery sculptures from the Northern Wei Dynasty, depicting a series of warriors. These pieces were associated with burials.

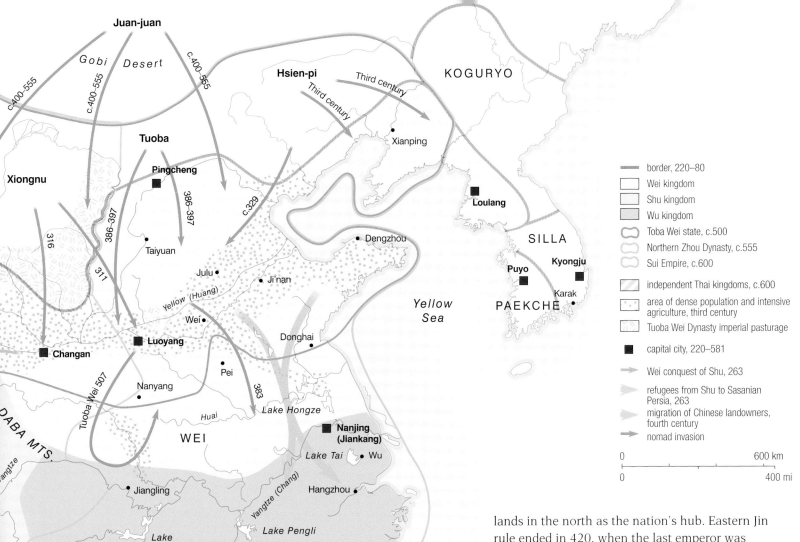

general, Fu Jian, briefly succeeded in reuniting all the northern lands, but his realm collapsed in 383. Meanwhile agricultural productivity plummeted, and the native Chinese were forced to seek safety by pledging their loyalty to feudal warlords.

It was a different story in the south. The Jin remained in power, ruling from the new capital of Jiankang (modern Nanjing). Their Eastern Jin kingdom attracted scholars and noble families fleeing the troubles in the north. Culture flourished, as did the economy, stimulated by the skills and wealth brought by the immigrants. The result was a lasting shift in China's geopolitical balance as the Yangtze (Chang) Valley challenged the Yellow (Huang) River

lands in the north as the nation's hub. Eastern Jin rule ended in 420, when the last emperor was smothered on the orders of a rebel general. Thereafter the south fell to a series of short-lived dynasties, each set up by military men. Meanwhile, the north was reunited from 440 on under the rule of the Tuoba, a once nomadic people who had assimilated Chinese ways.

Toward a united China

Historians often compare the collapse of northern China to the fall of the western Roman Empire at about the same date, but the long-term fate of the two powers was very different. The Tuoba established a dynasty along Chinese lines—the Northern Wei. From 471 Chinese again became the official language of the court, and Tuoba nobles adopted Chinese dress, manners, and even names. Before long the Tuoba and native Chinese populations were totally intermingled. Chinese culture survived, and there was no equivalent of the European Dark Ages.

The Northern Wei Dynasty was eventually brought down by court intrigue, and from 531 the north split again, this time into two competing kingdoms. The western dynasty finally prevailed over its eastern rival in 577, reuniting the region. Four years later a general of mixed Chinese and barbarian ancestry usurped the throne to proclaim the new Sui Dynasty. In 589 he subdued the south, reuniting China at last and bringing the long time of troubles to an end.

The Sui Dynasty

THE SHORT-LIVED SUI DYNASTY REUNITED A divided China but exhausted it in the process. Its roots lay in the mixed-race military aristocracy of the north. Its founder, Yang Jian, had a Chinese father and a Tatar mother.

Yang rose to prominence as a general. The Northern Zhou regime that he served controlled northwestern China in the late sixth century C.E., while the south was in the hands of the Chen. In 577 Yang led the Zhou forces to victory over a rival northern dynasty, the Northern Chi, reuniting the north. Four years later he seized power in his own name, killing the legitimate heir to the throne. He took the throne name of Wendi (Emperor Wen) and named his dynasty the Sui.

Wen's first task as ruler of northern China was to confront the Turks, who had created a steppe empire stretching as far as the Caspian Sea. He negotiated a peace treaty in 584 that secured his northern border. Then he looked to the south. After eliminating a small independent state in the middle Yangtze (Chang) Valley, he went on in 588 to invade the Chen lands. The southern armies put up little resistance. By the following year Wen had succeeded in reuniting China for the first time in almost 300 years.

Rebuilding and reforms

Wen turned his attention next to securing his gains. He razed the Chen capital of Jiankang, burning its palaces and temples and plowing up the streets to serve as farmland. For his own capital, he rebuilt the ancient city of Changan. He reestablished a unified administration for the nation as a whole. Taking the Han system as his model, he reorganized central and provincial government and revised the legal code. He also introduced reforms to give more land to the people who worked it, increasing agricultural output. On his death in 604 he bequeathed to his heir Yangdi a stable realm with an expanding population.

▲ Detail of an emperor with attendants from *Portraits of Thirteen Emperors*, attributed to the Tang Dynasty painter Yen Li-pen.

▶ The Grand Canal was Emperor Yangdi's greatest construction project. Running from Beijing in the north to Hangzhou in the south, it linked all the ancient canals between, including this one at Suzhou. The heavy boat traffic shows that canal transportation in China thrives to this day.

Yangdi squandered this legacy by ambition and extravagance. He used forced labor on a vast scale: more than 1 million men rebuilt the Great Wall, and 2 million constructed a new capital at Luoyang. Yangdi's greatest project, a Grand Canal (see pages 88–89) linking the Yangtze (Chang) Valley with the North China Plain by way of Luoyang, took 5 million men. The emperor celebrated its completion by sailing along it in a dragon boat 220 feet (65 m) long. The boat's central pavilion was four stories high and had a throne room decorated in jade and gold.

Determined to restore the nation's imperial glory, Yangdi began an aggressive foreign policy that made further demands on China's hard-pressed manpower. In 605 he restored Chinese sovereignty over northern Vietnam. He also laid plans to invade Taiwan and the southern Vietnamese kingdom of Champa.

His downfall came through his determination to conquer Koguryo, a northern kingdom that straddled southern Manchuria and northern Korea. In 612 he launched the first of three invasions, each as disastrous as the one before. Repeated military failure and the growing impoverishment of the realm sparked widespread revolts. In 616 the emperor was driven from northern China, which had suffered disproportionately in the Koguryo fiasco, to seek refuge in the south. Yet even there he was not safe. He was assassinated two years later, and with his death the Sui Dynasty came to an abrupt end.

▼ During the time of Emperor Yangdi dragon boats were lavishly equipped and decorated. Yangdi's own boat was four stories high and had more than 100 palatial rooms. Today dragon boats, such as this one on Kunming Lake, Beijing, are used to ferry passengers and tourists.

The Tang Dynasty

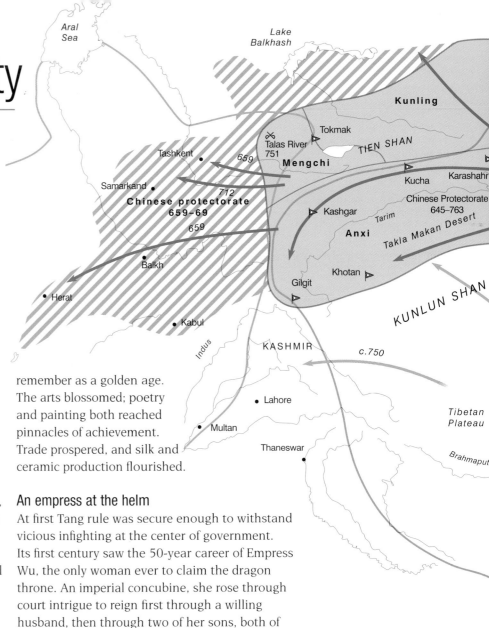

THE TANG DYNASTY ROSE FROM THE ASHES of the short-lived Sui regime in 617. In that year its founder Li Yuan, duke of Tang, seized the imperial capital of Changan and proclaimed himself emperor, taking the name of Gaozu. By 624 China was united under Tang control. Yet Gaozu had little time to enjoy his power. Two years later one of his sons staged a coup, killing his elder brother, the heir to the throne, and forcing Gaozu to abdicate. The young man then took power as Taizong. In a reign lasting 23 years, Taizong proved to be one of China's greatest emperors.

Gaozu and Taizong established a strong central administration that kept local governors in check. Inspectors reported back to the palace on conditions in the provinces. The civil service examination system, set up in Han times, was extended, broadening the pool from which the ruling class was drawn. Confucianism (see pages 60–61), with its emphasis on civic responsibility, was restored as the official ideology. Land redistribution was encouraged, increasing the number of peasant freeholders, whose taxes were the chief source of revenue.

The early Tang emperors also extended China's borders farther than ever before. In the west, imperial troops gained control of the Silk Road (see pages 26–27) all the way to the Tarim Basin and briefly into what is now Afghanistan. The northern state of Koguryo was finally conquered, although a new power, Silla, rose in its place to reclaim the Korean peninsula from Chinese rule.

The Tang heyday was a time of prosperity and political stability that later generations would remember as a golden age. The arts blossomed; poetry and painting both reached pinnacles of achievement. Trade prospered, and silk and ceramic production flourished.

An empress at the helm

At first Tang rule was secure enough to withstand vicious infighting at the center of government. Its first century saw the 50-year career of Empress Wu, the only woman ever to claim the dragon throne. An imperial concubine, she rose through court intrigue to reign first through a willing husband, then through two of her sons, both of whom she deposed. In 690 she eventually took power in her own name.

A more serious threat arose under Wu's grandson, Xuanzong. After a long reign that saw Tang power at its height, the emperor gradually withdrew from government to study Daoism (see pages 56–57), leaving the empire to spiral into crisis. In 751 Arab forces won the Battle of the Talas River, a defeat that cost China control of the western Silk Road.

Discontent leads to revolt

Also in 751, the Thai kingdom of Nanchao in the south defeated the Tang at the Battle of Dali, and in the north the Qidans threatened the border. Soon the newly united kingdom of Tibet began to challenge Tang authority. Rising taxes also caused discontent across the nation. It came to a head when An Lushan, a disaffected military leader, led 150,000 northern border troops against Changan in 756. Xuanzong had to flee for his life, and seven years passed before peace was restored.

The dynasty never recovered from the An Lushan revolt. Generals who took

▼ China's poets flourished under the Tang. Most of the emperors were patrons of poetry, and many were poets themselves. Li Bo, also known as Li Bai or Li Po, was one of the leading figures of Chinese poetry during the Tang period.

Tang Rulers			
617–626	Gaozu	779–805	Dezong
626–649	Taizong	805	Shunzong
649–683	Gaozong	805–820	Xianzong
684	Zhongzong	820–824	Muzong
684–690	Ruizong	824–827	Jingzong
690–705	Wu Zetian (Empress Wu)	827–840	Wenzong
		840–846	Wuzong
705–710	Zhongzong	846–859	Xuanzong
710–712	Ruizong	859–873	Yizong
712–756	Xuanzong	873–888	Xizong
756–762	Suzong	888–904	Zhaozong
762–779	Daizong	904–906	Aizong

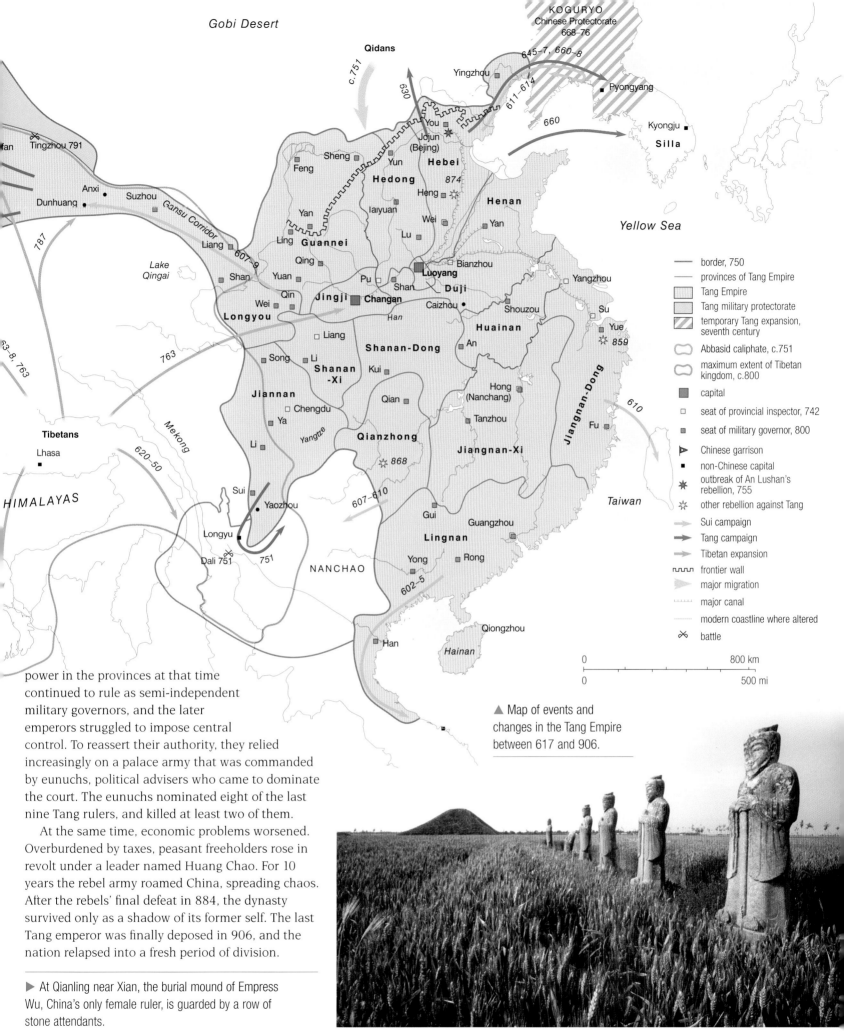

Gobi Desert

Qidans

KOGURYO
Chinese Protectorate
668–76

Yingzhou

645–7, 660–8

611–614

Pyongyang

630

Kyongju

You

Silla

660

Tingzhou 791

Jojun
(Bejing)

Anxi

Suzhou

Sheng

Yun

Hebei

Dunhuang

Gansu Corridor

Feng

Hedong

874

Henan

Yellow Sea

607–9

Yan

Heng

Iaiyuan

Wei

787

Liang

Ling

Guannei

Lu

Yan

Lake
Qingai

Qing

Yuan

Bianzhou

Shan

Pu

Shan

Luoyang

Yangzhou

Wei

Qin

Jingji

Changan

Duji

Longyou

Han

Caizhou

Shouzou

Su

Liang

Huainan

Yue
☼ 859

763

Song

Li

Shanan-Dong

An

Shanan
-Xi

Kui

Hong
(Nanchang)

Jiannan

Qian

Jiangnan-Dong

63–8, 763

Tibetans

Chengdu

Ya

Tanzhou

Fu

610

Lhasa

Mekong

Li

Yangtze

Qianzhong

Jiangnan-Xi

620–50

HIMALAYAS

☼ 868

Taiwan

Sui

Yaozhou

607–610

Longyu

Gui

Guangzhou

Dali 751

751

Lingnan

NANCHAO

Yong

Rong

602–5

Qiongzhou

Han

Hainan

border, 750
provinces of Tang Empire
Tang Empire
Tang military protectorate
temporary Tang expansion, seventh century
Abbasid caliphate, c.751
maximum extent of Tibetan kingdom, c.800
capital
seat of provincial inspector, 742
seat of military governor, 800
Chinese garrison
non-Chinese capital
outbreak of An Lushan's rebellion, 755
other rebellion against Tang
Sui campaign
Tang campaign
Tibetan expansion
frontier wall
major migration
major canal
modern coastline where altered
battle

0   800 km
0   500 mi

▲ Map of events and changes in the Tang Empire between 617 and 906.

power in the provinces at that time continued to rule as semi-independent military governors, and the later emperors struggled to impose central control. To reassert their authority, they relied increasingly on a palace army that was commanded by eunuchs, political advisers who came to dominate the court. The eunuchs nominated eight of the last nine Tang rulers, and killed at least two of them.

At the same time, economic problems worsened. Overburdened by taxes, peasant freeholders rose in revolt under a leader named Huang Chao. For 10 years the rebel army roamed China, spreading chaos. After the rebels' final defeat in 884, the dynasty survived only as a shadow of its former self. The last Tang emperor was finally deposed in 906, and the nation relapsed into a fresh period of division.

▶ At Qianling near Xian, the burial mound of Empress Wu, China's only female ruler, is guarded by a row of stone attendants.

A Time of Social Change

AFTER THE LONG PERIOD OF TROUBLES that followed the collapse of the Han Dynasty, the first decades of Tang rule saw the status quo restored. The balance of power in China had shifted southward under the Six Dynasties (see pages 28–29), when the north suffered repeated nomad invasions. Now the northern aristocrats were back in power. Gaozu and Taizong, the first Tang emperors, came from the ranks of the nobility, and they looked to their peers to help them rule.

Rise of the administrative class

That situation changed in later Tang and Song times. One reason was the growth of an administrative class, whose members rose to high official positions on their merit. Successive emperors used scholar-administrators from relatively humble backgrounds to break the grip of the old aristocracy—not just to lessen the threat to their own position, but for the good of the nation as a whole. The great landowners for the most part paid no taxes, and were in effect supported by the state.

The decline of the old ruling class was most apparent after An Lushan's revolt, which split the nation in the mid-eighth century (see pages 32–33). The rebellion coincided with a reduction of the population in the northeastern region—from half that of China as a whole in Sui times to little more

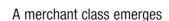

▲ Tang China created one of the greatest empires in the early medieval world. Merchants such as this furrier thronged the streets of the capital Changan.

than a third 150 years later. The south produced the nation's grain, and increased agricultural productivity resulted in crowded rural areas and booming cities.

As the emperors' authority weakened in the later Tang years, influence at court was increasingly in the hands of the eunuchs. They owed their positions not to birth but rather to court intrigue and physical proximity to the emperors. Meanwhile, power in the provinces devolved in many cases to local warlords who had risen through the ranks from lowly origins. This phenomenon was even more marked in the period known as the Five Dynasties that followed the Tang collapse, when the northern lands where the old aristocracy had their base were plunged into anarchy and strife (see pages 36–37).

A merchant class emerges

Another social trend that became evident under the Song Dynasty was the rise of the merchant class. Trade had traditionally been despised in China, and those who made their living by it had gained the disapproval of Confucius himself (see pages 60–61). The general prosperity enjoyed in Song times, however, brought huge riches to some traders. Many of these individuals used their wealth to buy land, blurring the borders between the new rich and the old landowning aristocracy. Meanwhile, officials of noble birth began to boost their incomes

the population of the big urban centers. By the mid-11th century, 10 of the largest Song conurbations each had more than 1 million inhabitants – at a time when the population of Paris, the largest city in northern Europe, probably numbered no more than 10,000.

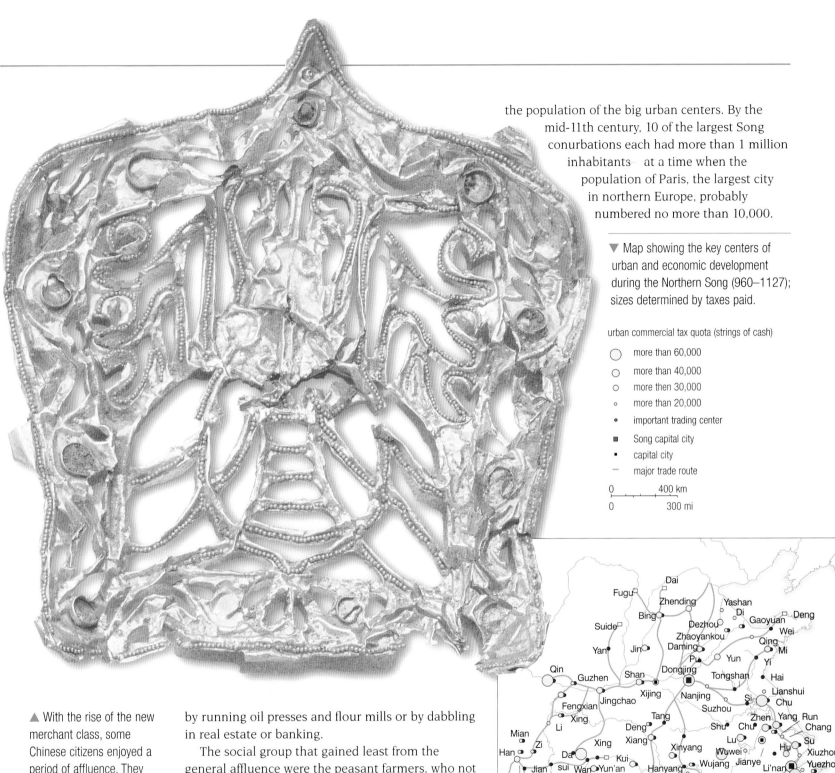

▼ Map showing the key centers of urban and economic development during the Northern Song (960–1127); sizes determined by taxes paid.

urban commercial tax quota (strings of cash)

○   more than 60,000
○   more than 40,000
○   more then 30,000
∘   more than 20,000
•   important trading center
■   Song capital city
▪   capital city
—   major trade route

0   400 km
0   300 mi

▲ With the rise of the new merchant class, some Chinese citizens enjoyed a period of affluence. They displayed their wealth by wearing fine ornaments and jewels such as this gold buckle.

◀ Women in the early Tang period enjoyed relatively high status and freedom. These figures are shown engaged in food production.

by running oil presses and flour mills or by dabbling in real estate or banking.

The social group that gained least from the general affluence were the peasant farmers, who not only fed the rest of society but also helped support it by paying a disproportionate share of the nation's taxes. Land redistribution schemes helped increase the number of small freeholders in early Tang times, but in the succeeding centuries the owner-farmers' lot gradually worsened until many were forced by economic necessity to sell their lands.

Large numbers chose to avoid the crippling burden of taxation by becoming tenants on the estates of large landowners or by taking work as hired hands. In practice, many became serfs in all but name. Other people moved to the cities, swelling

Five Dynasties, 10 Kingdoms

THERE ARE CYCLES IN CHINESE HISTORY. Strong dynasties collapse, giving way to periods of turmoil followed by fresh eras of stability and achievement. The period separating the Tang and Song dynasties was one such time of troubles, but it was brief, lasting just 54 years. Although many thousands died in internal strife, the break did little long-term harm to the nation as a whole, for the ideal of imperial unity survived, along with many of the Tang's administrative innovations. Chinese historians label this era the Five Dynasties and 10 Kingdoms.

Northern China—the five dynasties

The five dynasties were, in fact, a series of brief military dictatorships that successively ruled northern China. They saw a rapid succession of emperors—13 in all, from eight different families. Many had violent deaths: one was hanged, one burned to death in his own palace, one stabbed, another shot with arrows, and the list goes on. Chronologically, the three middle dynasties were Turkish in origin. Their rulers came from the small but influential Shatuo ethnic group, which had won a dominant position in the Chinese army. The final dynasty, the Later Zhou, restored Chinese rule and set about the tasks of reunification and reform that were eventually accomplished by the Song.

Two of the 10 kingdoms were, in fact, foreign-ruled realms established in frontier regions of the north. The Tanguts, a people of Tibetan origins, founded a small state in 1038, based around the Silk Road in northwestern China. It became the nucleus of the Buddhist kingdom of Xi Xia (Hsi-Hsia), which

▲ The ancient city of Jiaohe, situated along the old Silk Road, was built in the second century B.C.E. and prospered until the end of the Tang Dynasty. At its peak, it had an estimated population of 6,500. By the time of the Five Dynasties the city had begun to decline, and it was finally abandoned in the 14th century.

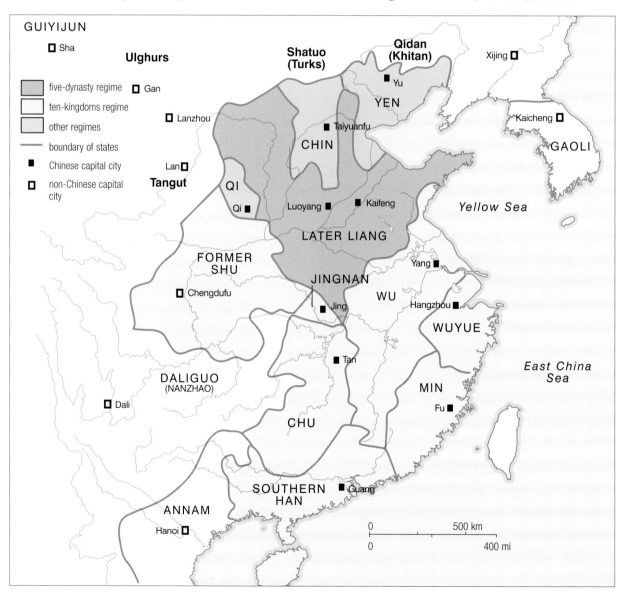

◀ Map of China in the Later Liang era (907–923), early in the period known as the Five Dynasties and 10 Kingdoms. In the first half of the 10th century, five dynasties occupying the northern central plain followed one another in rapid succession. In the south a total of 10 regimes came and went in the same period.

flourished until the Mongol invasions (see pages 40–41). Farther to the east the Qidans (Khitans) penetrated China's borders to set up the Liao realm, which survived until 1125. A Mongol people, they ruled from Yu (now Beijing). They adopted the Tang administrative system for their Chinese subjects, while applying tribal law among themselves. They lent their name of Khitai to Cathay, the term by which northern China was known to the West in Marco Polo's day.

The flourishing south

In the general breakdown of authority that followed the Tang collapse, southern China fragmented along geographical lines into separate kingdoms—their numbers varied from time to time. The shifting kingdoms that installed themselves there suffered far less economic disruption than the northern lands. Like their predecessors after the Han's demise, they benefited from an influx of fugitive northerners, boosting the population and bringing fresh talent. Some of these short-lived states flourished economically and culturally. One such was the Southern Tang kingdom (formerly the Wu) that occupied the modern provinces of Jiangsu, Anhui, and Jiangxi. Its able rulers expanded agricultural productivity by bringing former wasteland into cultivation. The capital of Nanjing became a center of learning and art.

With the coming of the Song Dynasty (see pages 38–39), much of the Tang system of government was restored. Yet some things had changed over the years, and different cities had risen to prominence. The Song capital of Kaifeng had already served as the home of the earlier Later Liang Dynasty, while Hangzhou, which would one day host the Southern Song emperors, had housed the rulers of the southern kingdom of Wuyue.

The north was the main loser from the changes. In economic terms it fell behind the south, which was increasingly the nation's breadbasket and the center of its prosperity. The Tangut and Qidan enclaves remained, reducing the area under imperial control and providing a constant threat to national security. Most significantly of all, perhaps, the Turkish irruption had cost the old northern nobility its commanding position in affairs of state. As the meritocratic culture of the Song would prove, the era of aristocratic domination of government had gone for good.

The Five Dynasties and the Ten Kingdoms

Period	Dynasty	Years
Five Dynasties (occupying central plain)	Later Liang Dynasty	**907–923** (17 years)
	Later Tang Dynasty (Shatuo Turk)	**923–936** (13 years)
	Later Jin Dynasty	**936–946** (10 years)
	Later Han Dynasty	**947–950** (3 years)
	Later Zhou Dynasty	**951–960** (10 years)
Ten Kingdoms (mostly occupying southern China)	Wu kingdom	**920–937** (17 years)
	Wuyue kingdom	**907–978** (72 years)
	Southern Han kingdom	**907–971** (65 years)
	Chu kingdom	**907–951** (45 years)
	Former Shu kingdom	**907–925** (18 years)
	Min kingdom	**909–945** (35 years)
	Jingnan kingdom	**924–963** (40 years)
	Later Shu kingdom	**934–965** (32 years)
	Southern Tang kingdom (formerly Wu)	**937–975** (39 years)
	Northern Han kingdom (on northern border)	**937–979** (29 years)
Liao	Liao Dynasty	**907–1125** (218 years)

The Song Dynasty

THE FIRST SONG EMPEROR SEIZED POWER over northern China in 960 in a relatively bloodless military coup. Having brought the various southern kingdoms to heel as much by diplomacy as by armed force, he then persuaded his leading generals to resign their posts in return for honors and extensive estates. By his actions he set the tone for the Song years, which brought China a prolonged spell of prosperity and peace.

At a time when most of the world was ruled by brute force, China enjoyed a flourishing culture and an expanding economy. Agricultural production soared thanks to the introduction from Champa (today's southern Vietnam) of a new strain of rice that permitted two crops to be grown each year.

The population also mushroomed, from 60 million early in the 11th century to more than 100 million by 1124. Meanwhile, the empire experienced something approaching an industrial revolution. By the mid-11th century, China was producing 14 times more iron, 13 times more silver, and eight times as much copper as in Tang times two centuries earlier.

The "New Laws"

Yet the Song years also saw a growing budget deficit, caused partly by tax evasion by large landowners and partly by spiraling expenditure on a huge standing army. Arguments over how best to address the problem caused the biggest political crisis of the 11th century. In the 1070s a minister named Wang Anshi introduced a comprehensive reform program. His New Laws addressed everything from the civil service exam curriculum (where he introduced engineering and medicine alongside the traditional academic

subjects) to horse-breeding projects to supply the imperial cavalry.

Wang reinstated village militias (armed forces) to reduce the state's dependence on the standing army. He also commissioned a fresh land survey to update the tax system, and introduced low-interest government loans to help peasant farmers. Such measures, though, not only threatened the vested interests of the influential landed class but also offended conservative Confucian scholars, who were always suspicious of innovation in general and of big government in particular. As a result, the laws were only applied in a piecemeal fashion, and the problems continued to fester.

Song China's main weakness was its relations with its northern neighbors. The Qidan and Tangut states that had been established under the Five Dynasties (see pages 36–37) were a thorn in China's side. At first the government tried to buy its way out of trouble. After a military defeat in 1004 the Qidan demanded an annual tribute of 100,000 ounces (2,835 kg) of silver and 200,000 bolts of silk. The Tanguts won a similar concession 40 years later. This arrangement, costing 2 percent of China's annual income, effectively secured peace for a century.

The system finally broke down in the 12th century when a new power, the Jürchen, established a state on the Qidans' northern border. Seeking to play the two "barbarian" peoples off against one another,

▲ Painting and other art forms flourished under the Song Dynasty. This portrait is of Emperor Gaozong (ruled 1127–62).

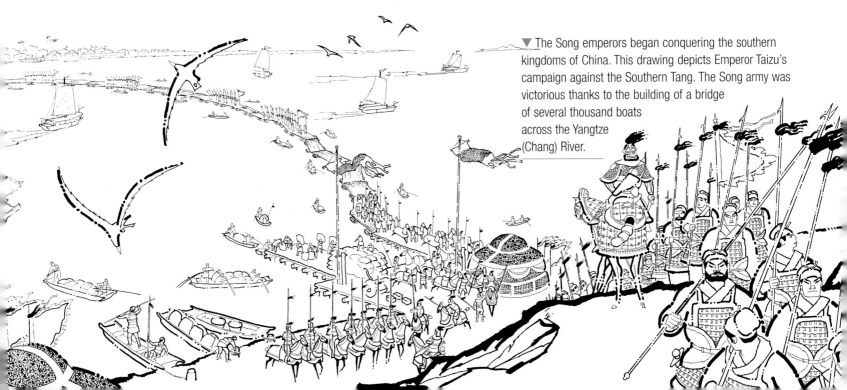

▼ The Song emperors began conquering the southern kingdoms of China. This drawing depicts Emperor Taizu's campaign against the Southern Tang. The Song army was victorious thanks to the building of a bridge of several thousand boats across the Yangtze (Chang) River.

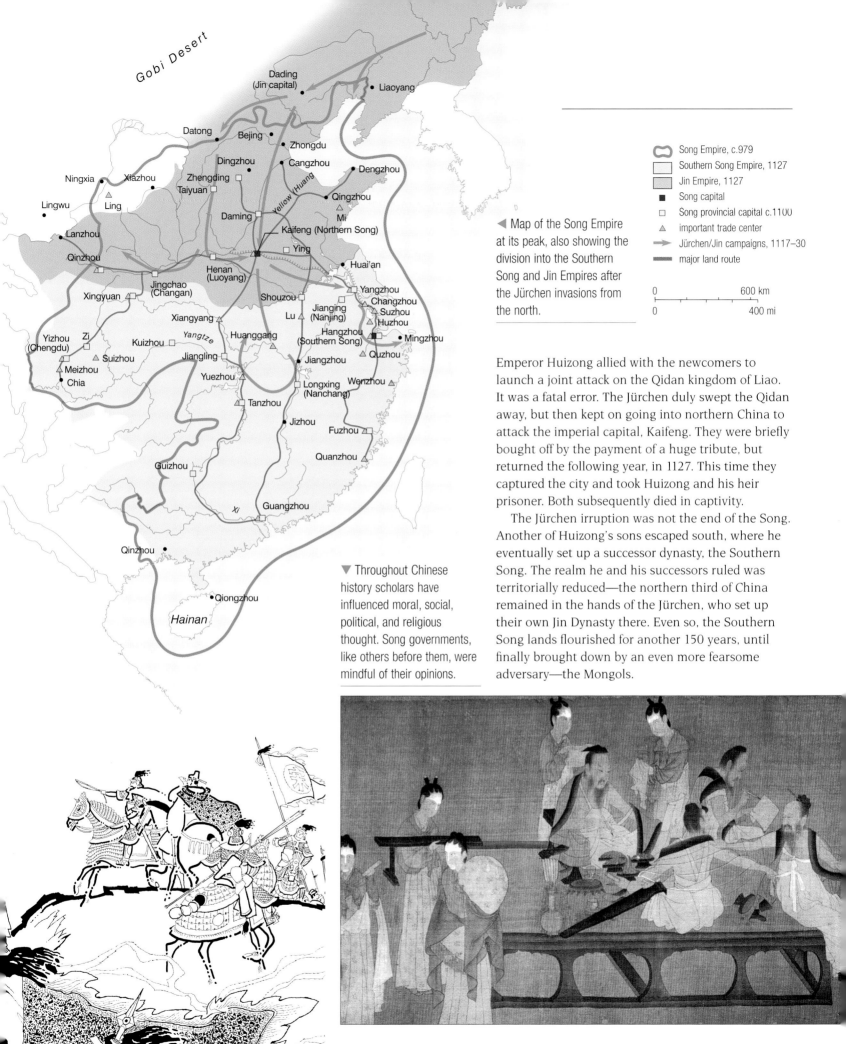

Gobi Desert

Dading
(Jin capital)

Liaoyang

Datong Bejing

Zhongdu

Ningxia Xiazhou Zhengding
Dingzhou
Cangzhou

Dengzhou

Lingwu Ling
Taiyuan

Qingzhou

Lanzhou
Daming Mi

Yellow (Huang)

Qinzhou
Kaifeng (Northern Song)

Ying

Huai'an

Henan
(Luoyang)

Jingchao (Changan)

Yangzhou

Xingyuan Shouzou
Changzhou

Jianging Suzhou
Lu (Nanjing)

Xiangyang
Huzhou

Yizhou Zi Kuizhou Huanggang
Hangzhou
(Chengdu) Jiangling (Southern Song)

Mingzhou

Suizhou Yuezhou Jiangzhou
Meizhou Quzhou
Chia

Longxing Wenzhou
Yangtze (Nanchang)

Tanzhou

Jizhou

Fuzhou

Guizhou Quanzhou

Xi Guangzhou

Qinzhou

Qiongzhou

Hainan

◻ Song Empire, c.979
◻ Southern Song Empire, 1127
◻ Jin Empire, 1127
■ Song capital
◻ Song provincial capital c.1100
△ important trade center
→ Jürchen/Jin campaigns, 1117–30
━ major land route

0   600 km
0   400 mi

◀ Map of the Song Empire at its peak, also showing the division into the Southern Song and Jin Empires after the Jürchen invasions from the north.

▼ Throughout Chinese history scholars have influenced moral, social, political, and religious thought. Song governments, like others before them, were mindful of their opinions.

Emperor Huizong allied with the newcomers to launch a joint attack on the Qidan kingdom of Liao. It was a fatal error. The Jürchen duly swept the Qidan away, but then kept on going into northern China to attack the imperial capital, Kaifeng. They were briefly bought off by the payment of a huge tribute, but returned the following year, in 1127. This time they captured the city and took Huizong and his heir prisoner. Both subsequently died in captivity.

The Jürchen irruption was not the end of the Song. Another of Huizong's sons escaped south, where he eventually set up a successor dynasty, the Southern Song. The realm he and his successors ruled was territorially reduced—the northern third of China remained in the hands of the Jürchen, who set up their own Jin Dynasty there. Even so, the Southern Song lands flourished for another 150 years, until finally brought down by an even more fearsome adversary—the Mongols.

The Mongol Invasion

OVER THE CENTURIES CHINA WAS INVADED repeatedly by nomadic peoples from the north—as early as the third century B.C.E. the First Emperor built the Great Wall to keep just such intruders out. Even so, nothing quite prepared the nation for the Mongol incursions of the 13th century. Genghis Khan, who led the assault, practiced a new kind of total warfare, using terror and destruction as deliberate instruments of policy. His maxim was that "the greatest joy is to conquer one's enemies, to pursue them, to seize their belongings, to see their families in tears, to ride their horses, to possess their wives and daughters."

The first inkling of trouble came in 1206, with the news that a leader named Temujin had united the warring clans of the Mongolian steppes and had been proclaimed Genghis Khan ("Universal Ruler") of all the Mongol peoples. The following year Genghis led his first foreign campaign, against the Tangut kingdom of Xi Xia, established under the Five Dynasties (see pages 36–37). Progress

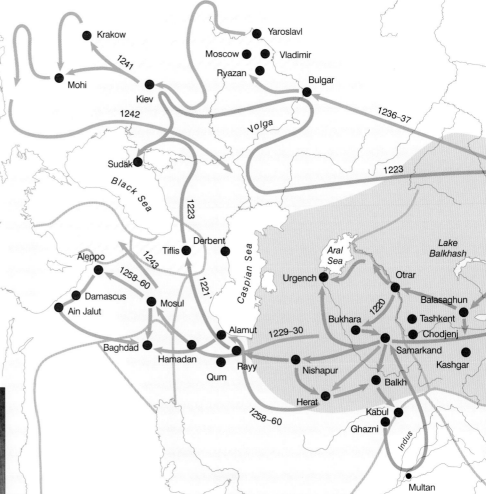

was slowed by the Mongols' lack of siege-engines to force walled towns into submission. Even so, Xi Xia was overcome by 1209, and its ruler was forced to pay tribute.

Genghis's next target was the Jin Kingdom of the Qidan, which had ruled northern China since 1127. This time the conqueror took care to acquire the assistance of siege-engineers, many of them Chinese. Zhongdu, the imperial capital, finally fell in 1215 and was reduced to ruins, and most of its inhabitants

◄ Genghis Khan, 1167–1227. Although today Genghis is considered by many in the West to have been a bloodthirsty conqueror, he is celebrated in Mongolia as a hero and father of the Mongol nation.

▼ Map showing the Mongol campaigns of the 13th century. They swept out of the Asian steppes to terrorize the settled peoples of Eurasia. Genghis Khan first invaded China, then turned his attention to central Asia and Europe. After further Mongol campaigns in China, it was Kublai Khan who finally conquered the Southern Song kingdom.

0   800 km
0   500 mi

TIEN SHAN
1218
Karakorum
Gobi Desert
1234
1211, 1215
JIN KINGDOM
Liaoyang
1215
1231–60
1209
1236, 1241
1226–27
1209
1209
Zhongdu
Kaegyong
Tonggyong
XI XIA KINGDOM
Datong
Yellow
1213–14
Dengzhou
Laizhou
YELLOW SEA
Takla Makan Desert
Ningxia
Taiyuan
Pingyang
1818
Jining
1281
1227
Kaifeng
Huazhou
Zaizhou
KUNLUN SHAN
1236, 1251
1236
Xiangyang
1236
Hangzhou
Tibetan Plateau
Yangtze
SONG KINGDOM
Lhasa
Chengdu
Brahmaputra
Jianzhou
HIMALAYAS
1253
1258
Ganges
Dali
NAN CHAO
1257
Wuzhou
Guangzhou
1277
Mekong
ANNAM
1281
Pagan
Daluo

Kublai Khan's advance on the south

were slaughtered. For a time Genghis even considered wiping out much of the population of northern China. He was dissuaded by an adviser named Yelu Chucai, himself a Qidan, who convinced him that the Mongols' long-term interests would be better served by letting the bulk of the population live to pay taxes and supply food for their armies.

After the fall of Zhongdu, Genghis turned his attention westward to central Asia and Europe, leaving the task of mopping up remaining pockets of resistance to one of his generals. Twenty years went by before the Mongols looked toward the unconquered south. By that time Genghis was dead, and supreme power had passed to his son, Ogedei. Even then the new Great Khan finally decided to concentrate on other targets, realizing that the canals and paddy fields of southern China were difficult terrain for the Mongol cavalry.

Kublai Khan's advance on the south

The leader who finally took up the challenge was Kublai Khan, grandson of Genghis Khan. Kublai was very different from his predecessors. He was literate, having received a Chinese education, and he spent most of his life in China rather on the steppes. When he was proclaimed Great Khan in 1264, his accession triggered a split in the Mongol ranks. For traditionalists he was too Chinese, and they took up arms against him, only to be defeated in battle.

Kublai built a fleet ahead of his assault on the southern lands. He was also able to call on Chinese and Qidan troops from the north to carry out the invasion. Even so, it took almost three decades to break the Southern Song resistance. By 1271 Kublai felt sure enough of ultimate success to proclaim the creation of a new Mongol dynasty, the Yuan. Eight years later his troops finally defeated the surviving remnants of the old imperial forces in a sea battle.

The conquest had taken a long time—68 years—but after 1279 it was to all intents and purposes complete. China was reunited again as one small part of a huge Mongol empire that stretched west across much of the Eurasian landmass, as far as the Mediterranean Sea and the Danube River. But the nation also found itself under foreign rule, and although the Mongol peace brought a revival of trade, few of the benefits flowed into Chinese hands or pockets.

China Under the Mongols

CHINA HAD EXPERIENCED FOREIGN RULE many times before the Mongol conquest, but it had never before been so harsh. To start with, the Mongols had seized the whole country, not just the north as earlier invaders had done. The newcomers also failed to adopt Chinese ways. Instead, they formed a small, foreign military elite, clustered around Beijing and south along the Grand Canal as far as the central city of Nanjing.

Under their rule, the nation's population divided into four different groups, ranked in a clear order of hierarchy. The Mongols themselves were at the top, and were a largely parasitical presence. Being poorly equipped for the task of governing, they chose their administrators from a second class of foreigners, known as the *semuren*, or "people with colored eyes." Composed mainly of Turks, Persians, and Arabs from the Mongol-ruled lands to the west, these people were considered reliable because they were wholly dependent on Mongol favor—they thrived as merchants and entrepreneurs as well as civil servants. The third group consisted of subjects of the former Qidan lands in northern China, who were marginally preferred to the last of the four, the native Chinese who had been loyal to the Southern Song.

The top two groups enjoyed tax exemptions and other privileges, but the native Chinese were penalized in various ways. They were forbidden to learn the Mongol language, bear arms, or go out after dark. Their greatest burden was heavy taxation. The peasantry not only supported the luxurious lifestyle of their foreign rulers but also had to pay for their military exploits, notably a series of campaigns waged in Southeast Asia and against Japan (see map on page 41). Few of the ventures succeeded, for the military strengths of the Mongols were not suited to the tropical conditions of the southern lands or (in the case of Japan) naval warfare.

▼ Under Mongol (Yuan) rule Chinese scholars found it difficult to enter official careers (partly because of examination quotas, which were set on a racial basis), and many turned instead to art and drama. The drawing illustrates the staging of a *zaju* ("variety") play. The ruling Mongol class ride by as the local Han people watch the play.

▶ Kublai Khan proclaimed the creation of a new Mongol dynasty, the Yuan, in 1271. Although he embarked on programs to improve China's economy and infrastructure, his policies brought great hardship to many people.

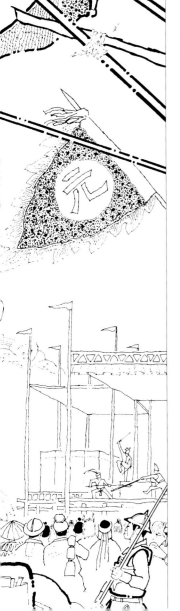

caused the Grand Canal, China's chief transportation artery, to silt up. As famine spread, so did discontent. The White Lotus sect, a movement that combined Buddhist and Daoist ideas, sponsored armed revolt by rebel bands who became known as the Red Turbans because of their distinctive headgear.

Ousted by rebels

The Mongol emperors fought back, suppressing the Red Turbans by 1362. By that time, however, other rebels had seized large swaths of south and central China. The most successful, a peasant and onetime Buddhist monk named Zhu Yuanzhang, built up a power base around Nanjing, from which he gradually overcame rival insurgent warlords. By 1367 he was strong enough to oppose the Yuan (Mongol) rulers themselves, sending an army of 250,000 men to attack Beijing. The capital fell in the following year, and the last Mongol ruler fled back to Mongolia. Zhu proclaimed a new dynasty, the Ming, and China was back in Chinese hands at last.

Mongol rule had lasted for less than a century. It left some permanent traces, among them an improved road system and the transfer of the imperial capital to Beijing, near the nation's northern border. For the most part, though, it was a foreign imposition that failed to take root, and it was rejected as soon as the Chinese were once more strong enough to overthrow it.

Kublai himself was strong enough to impose his will, but political instability followed his death in 1294, as 10 different emperors held the throne over the next 40 years. Meanwhile, the suffering of China's peasants was made worse by the natural disasters that continued to afflict the nation.

A first wave of rebellion broke out in 1337, and was harshly suppressed. Then in 1344 the Yellow (Huang) River burst its banks, and the flooding

▶ Mongol ambition knew no bounds. As well as invading China, Kublai Khan sent Mongol fleets to launch unsuccessful attacks on Japan in 1274 and 1281. This 19th-century Japanese engraving depicts the destruction of the second fleet by a *kamikaze*, or "divine wind" (in fact, a typhoon).

The Ming Dynasty

ZHU YUANZHANG, THE PEASANT REBEL who succeeded in driving the Mongols out of China in 1368 (see pages 42–43), had no ancestral title for which he could name his dynasty. Instead, he called it the Ming (meaning "brilliant"). He also revived the practice of designating his reign by a throne title—in his case Hongwu ("Boundless Martial Valor"). As a result, he is usually referred to in Western sources as the Hongwu emperor, a style that is also applied to his imperial successors. More conveniently, but less correctly, he is also often called simply Hongwu.

A return to Chinese values

The revolt against foreign overlords such as the Mongols had had its roots in Chinese nationalism, and one of the emperor's first concerns was to

▲ The Mongols used paper and silver as money, but the Ming reintroduced bronze coins. The square hole was used for stringing coins together.

Ming Rulers	
1368–1398	Zhu Yuanzhang (Hongwu)
1399–1402	Jianwen
1402–1424	Yongle
1424–1425	Hongxi
1426–1435	Xuande
1436–1449	Zhengtong
1450–1457	Jingtai
1457–1464	Tianshun
1465–1487	Chenghua
1488–1505	Hongzhi
1506–1521	Zhengde
1522–1567	Jiahing
1567–1572	Longqing
1573–1620	Wanli
1620	Taichang
1621–1627	Tianqi
1628–1644	Zhongzhen

restore the ancient traditions that the Mongols had put aside.

The old imperial rites were revived, and Confucianism (see pages 60–61) came back into favor at court. In time the civil service examinations were also reinstated, although Hongwu, being a man of action rather than words, insisted on including horsemanship and archery in the syllabus (albeit briefly). A nationwide network of state-supported schools was set up to recruit potential candidates. Students who won through to gain government jobs were given Tang-era uniforms, in homage to what was now seen as a golden age of Chinese greatness.

Economic reforms

The most important priority, however, was to restore the nation's economic health, which had suffered very badly in the last decades of Mongol rule. The situation was particularly severe in northern China, so Hongwu forcibly resettled homeless families from the south to reclaim abandoned land there. He also undertook a number of ambitious irrigation and drainage projects, and had more than a billion trees planted nationwide to provide fruit and shade.

New crops were introduced, among them Indian corn, peanuts, and sweet potatoes, while crop rotation was improved. Increased agricultural productivity in the Ming years supported a demographic upsurge that saw the nation's population once more pass the 100 million mark, regaining the level of Song times (see pages 38–39).

Hongwu also took steps to put the imperial finances back in order. The Mongol practice of allowing local officials—who were often corrupt— to collect taxes was dropped in favor of a centralized system. A new census and land survey also helped update revenue collection. At the same time, the army was strengthened to counter the continuing Mongol threat, and new frontier lands were brought under Ming control (see pages 46–47). Even so, much had changed since Tang times, and despite its name the Ming era never quite managed to recapture the brilliance of the earlier age.

One continuing weakness was the tradition of autocratic rule that Hongwu himself established. Always suspicious of rivals, he became increasingly paranoid in the course of his 30-year reign, and ordered a series of purges that cost the lives of many of his closest and most able aides.

The situation improved little under his successors. The third Ming emperor, Yongle, was a brilliant general who raised the dynasty to a military peak. Yet by choosing in 1421 to move the capital from Hongwu's base of Nanjing back to Beijing near the northern border, he physically removed himself from China's economic heart. Isolated within the newly built Forbidden City (see pages 86–87), successive emperors had little contact with their subjects and were increasingly cocooned from the outside world by an entourage of eunuch servants.

The closed, conservative world of the imperial court could not check the economic vibrancy of the early Ming period, but it ultimately had an inhibiting effect on the nation's culture. The early Ming years

saw great naval expeditions dispatched across the southern oceans, but these ceased from 1433, after which the nation increasingly turned in on itself.

Signs of decline

The time-honored arts of poetry and painting stagnated, as did the study of philosophy, and only new media such as drama and the novel flourished. Worse still, China for the first time lost its technological edge. In the vital skill of gunmaking it fell behind the emergent European powers, whose sailors ventured to China's shores from the early 16th century. Under the Ming China still saw itself as the hub of global civilization, but in fact other parts of the world were rapidly catching up.

▲ A 16th-century painting from the Ming era portrays an official and his wife. Under Ming rule, the role of educated officials in running the government was restored.

Expansion of the Empire

UNDER THE EARLY MING EMPERORS China's frontiers expanded beyond their limits under the Tang. Some of the gains were lands first conquered by the Mongols that had remained part of China when the Yuan Dynasty was expelled. One such was the Liaodong Peninsula adjoining Korea, which became permanently joined to the empire.

The emperors also won control of the southwestern region of Yunnan, which in Tang and Song times was part of the Thai kingdom of Nanchao. Yunnan fell to Kublai Khan's forces in the 1250s, and was ruled as a semi-independent Mongol fief. It eventually fell to the armies of the Hongwu emperor in 1382, and thereafter became an integral part of China, remaining so to the present day.

Northern raids and ocean exploration

In the north the Mongols continued to present a threat. In 1372 Hongwu sent an army across the Gobi Desert to Genghis Khan's old capital of Karakorum, which was burned to the ground. The force then advanced across the Yablonovy Mountains into what is now southern Russia—the farthest

north any Chinese expedition had ever penetrated. Twenty-four years later the emperor again sent troops north of the Great Wall, foiling a threatened invasion before the clans had time to fully gather.

The emperor's son, Zhu, who commanded that foray, took the throne as Yongle in 1402. He led five more incursions into Mongol territory over the next two decades. In 1409 he sent a huge force of half a million men to the northwestern borderlands, where a number of small states had sprung up in the wake of the Yuan collapse. Even so, the Ming never succeeded in imposing their grip on the Silk Road as their Tang predecessors had done.

In the early expansionist years, the Ming emperors showed greater interest in the maritime trade routes of the China Sea and the Indian Ocean. Between 1405 and 1433, seven naval expeditions were launched, commanded by Admiral Zheng He. They reached the shores of East Africa, the Persian Gulf, and the Red Sea.

One purpose was to spread the fame of the Ming, whose authority was more widely acknowledged than that of any of their predecessors—even the Mameluke rulers of Egypt sent an envoy to Beijing.

▲ A solitary stone tortoise marks the site of Karakorum, Genghis Khan's capital, which was burned to the ground by the Ming in 1372. Passers-by drop stones on the turtle as a kind of prayer. Behind the statue is a row of stupas (Buddhist shrines).

Legend:
- —— state border, c.1590
- ▢ Ming territory, c.1590
- ▢ Ming tributary or buffer state, c.1590
- —— Chinese trade route
- ∿∿∿ Great Wall

Hami, Anxi, Suzhou, Ganzhou, Liangzhou, Xining, Lanzhou, Ningxia, Yulin, Datong, Kalgan, Beijing, Shanhaiguan, Jinzhou, Shenyang (Mukden), Kaiyuan, Liaoyang, Haizhou, LIAODONG, Wonsan, Pyongyang, Seoul, CHAOXIN (KOREA), Ulsan, Pusan, Dengzhou, Pingdu, Jinan, SHANDONG, Huaian, Yellow Sea, Rehe, Taiyuan, ZHILI, SHANXI, SHAANXI, Kaifeng, HENAN, Changan, Fengxian, Guangyuan, Chamdo, SICHUAN, Wushan, Chengdu, Jingzhou, HUGUANG, Wuchang, Nanjing, NANZHILI, Hangzhou, Mingzhou (Ningbo), ZHEJIANG, Wenzhou, East China Sea, Chongqing, Luzhou, Nanchang, Tanzhou, Jujiang, JIANGXI, Yuanling, Zhaotong, Hengzhou, Tingzhou, Ganzhou, Fuzhou, FUJIAN, Jilong, Guiyang, GUIZHOU, Zhangzhou, Xiamen (Amoy), Tainan, Dali, Yunnan, Menghua, Guilin, GUANGXI, GUANGDONG, Guangzhou (Canton), YUNNAN

0 — 800 km
0 — 600 mi

◄ Map showing the extent of the Ming Empire in 1590.

More practically, the voyages aimed to stimulate trade, often masquerading in the form of tribute. Zheng He bestowed lavish gifts on all the rulers who received him, and the Ming expected equally generous offerings in return, choosing to view them as a form of homage to their own exalted rule.

The situation changed radically from the mid-15th century on, when the emperors ordered ocean voyages to be halted. The cost was proving prohibitive at a time when the state treasury was already stretched. Instead, the emperors encouraged internal trade. They extended and improved the Grand Canal (see pages 88–89), which once again became the nation's main commercial artery. Another factor in their decision was an upsurge in coastal piracy. By 1525 it was an offense for a private individual to own a boat with more than one mast.

The decision to abandon ocean exploration— known to historians as the Great Withdrawal—was to have profound significance. China turned its back on maritime expansion only a few decades before the European mariners of the Age of Exploration opened up the world's seas. A first Portuguese vessel arrived on China's coast in 1513, within 15 years of Vasco da Gama's pioneering voyage to India. The Chinese

authorities discouraged the early contacts, partly because of the piratical behavior of the newcomers, who viewed their hosts as heathens fit for plundering rather than as equal trading partners. But they could not keep them out entirely. By turning their back on the sea, they effectively condemned China in centuries to come to humiliation at the hands of foreign navies that grew in power and reach at the same time as their own forces shrank.

◀ A small river junk, with typical blunt bow, rudder, and folding sail. The network of canals and inland waterways that criss-crossed China was already more than 30,000 miles (48,000 km) long in the Song period, and it grew even more extensive in late imperial times. The Chinese also made use of coastal routes for carrying goods.

Downfall of the Ming

IN 1449, 81 YEARS AFTER THE MING DYNASTY was founded, the Zhengtong Emperor, a young man just 22 years of age, led an army beyond the Great Wall, which ran barely 50 miles (80 km) north of the imperial capital of Beijing. His force was ambushed there by a Mongol horde that decimated the troops and took the emperor himself captive.

The Mongols were not strong enough at the time to take Beijing, although they reached its suburbs. Zhengtong was eventually released from captivity and resumed the throne after an eight-year gap. Yet the incident had shown up the dynasty's vulnerability and a fundamental flaw in its structure. The emperor had ventured out against the advice of his generals at the urging of a court favorite, a eunuch named Wang Zheng who was himself killed in the battle.

The number of eunuchs mushroomed as the years passed, from 10,000 early in the 16th century to 100,000 immediately before the dynasty's fall. The courtiers used their influence to distract emperors from affairs of state—some later rulers never met with their ministers or bothered to read official dispatches. The eunuchs filled the resulting power vacuum, turning it to their own advantage. One corrupt imperial favorite amassed a personal fortune equating to 7,700 tons (7,000 tonnes) of silver, not to mention a treasure in gold plate and jewels.

Treasury in crisis

Meanwhile, the state treasury was depleted, not just by court extravagance but by revenues that failed to keep up with expenditure. Income from overseas trade dwindled as China reduced its foreign ties. Agriculture was dominated by large landowners who were strong enough to resist the demands of government tax collectors. As a result, an increasing burden fell on a dwindling number of peasant farmers, who grew steadily more and more impoverished as the dynasty progressed.

The government's greatest financial commitment was the need to maintain a strong army. Throughout the Ming years, China's borders were under pressure. In the north, the Mongols remained a threat. Pirates operating out of Japan and from offshore islands plagued the nation's coasts, requiring a sizeable military presence to counter their raids.

In addition, a fresh danger loomed in the late 16th century, after new military rulers took power in Japan. In 1592 and again in 1597, the Japanese warlord Hideyoshi sent huge armadas to invade Korea, a client kingdom of the Ming. In each case

the invaders were beaten back, but only at a cost that the imperial treasury could ill afford.

Another threat was gathering force in the northeast. The Manchus were a branch of the Jürchen people who had invaded Song China in the 12th century, establishing the Jin Dynasty in the northern lands (see pages 38–39). Under a dynamic leader named Nurhaci they now extended their grip over the region known today as Manchuria, which then lay just beyond China's northeastern border. By the time of Nurhaci's death in 1626 they had penetrated the Chinese frontier and had established a new capital at Mukden, within Ming territory.

Internal chaos

It was internal collapse that ultimately brought down the Ming. A series of natural disasters—droughts, famines, and floods—sparked peasant revolts across the nation from 1627 on. In 1644 the strongest of the rebel armies seized Beijing itself, and the last Ming emperor hanged himself in the grounds of the Forbidden City. The Manchus took advantage of the ensuing chaos to march on Beijing. By the end of 1644, the peasant rebels were on the run, and foreign rulers were once more installed in the capital. The Ming had been replaced by the Manchu Qing Dynasty, which would rule for the next 268 years.

▲ Thirty miles (50 km) northwest of Beijing stands a group of hills. Each of the 13 Ming emperors is buried at the foot of a different hill. The area, known as the Ming Tombs, stretches for 15 square miles (40 sq. km).

◀ This drawing of a peasant uprising in Ming times shows serfs burning their bonds of servitude in the courtyard of their landlord's house. The landlord is tied to a pillar (center) and flogged, while serfs carry off grain and silk as booty.

Part Two

Culture and
Society

▲ A statue of the Buddha, one of more than 50,000 stone figures that have been found carved into the mountainside at Yungang Grottoes, Shanxi province.

▶ Detail taken from the painting *The Qing Ming Festival by the Riverside,* created in the 12th century by Zhang Zeduan and showing the Song capital of Kaifeng.

The Lie of the Land

CHINA'S FIRST URBAN CIVILIZATION GOT under way in the north of the country, around the middle reaches of the Yellow (Huang) River. The setting—a land of harsh blizzards and fierce winters—was an unlikely one. The region's saving grace was its soil, composed of loess particles carried by the wind from the Gobi Desert 600 miles (1,000 km) away and deposited in a blanket up to 450 feet (135 m) deep. The grainy loess was easy to work, even with primitive digging sticks, and was very fertile. Here early farmers grew millet and wheat, joined from the second millennium B.C.E. on by soybeans, which improve soil fertility by enriching it with nitrates.

The loess was carried downstream by the Yellow River, which took its name from the color the soil particles gave it. In its lower reaches the river meandered across a vast plain, dropping no more than 6 inches (15 cm) in the last 500 miles (800 km) of its course to the sea. Silting of the riverbed steadily raised the water level until the river actually ran above the level of the surrounding plain, restrained only by its banks, which had to be raised artificially to prevent flooding.

Even so, these artificial levees (embankments) were often breached, causing devastating floods. Historians have calculated that the river has overflowed its banks 1,500 times in the last 3,000 years, claiming more than 10 million lives and winning it the name of "China's sorrow." Yet there is also a positive side to the floods. They spread fertile silt across the coastal plain, creating another rich area for the survivors to exploit.

The southern ricebasket

Southern China is a very different land, hotter and more moist than the dry, windswept north. The dividing line is the Yangtze (Chang) River, third longest in the world after the Nile and the Amazon. To the south of the Yangtze a different kind of agriculture flourishes, based on rice, which was first domesticated from wild strains that grew in the delta region 6,000 years ago.

In those early days the subtropical lands of the southeast were heavily forested, but once the trees were cleared they became hugely productive. Rice paddies spread to cover the land, creating the landscape most foreigners think of when they imagine China. By the seventh century C.E. this region had become the ricebasket of China, supplying surplus grain to feed the less prolific north.

▲ Much of northern China is made up of arid land, with two of the world's harshest deserts—the Gobi in the northeast and the Takla Makan (shown here)—in the northwest.

By that time a north–south divide had developed, with economic power concentrated in the south, thanks both to the fertile land and to busy ports serving the trade networks of the South China Sea. But political power was exercised from the north, where the country's capital lay—from Ming times at Beijing, near the northern border with Manchuria.

An even deeper division separated the lands of Inner China, north and south, from the vast expanses of Outer China—the sparsely inhabited territories that lay beyond the frontiers of the early Chinese kingdoms, to be gradually brought within the nation's cultural and political boundaries. Inner

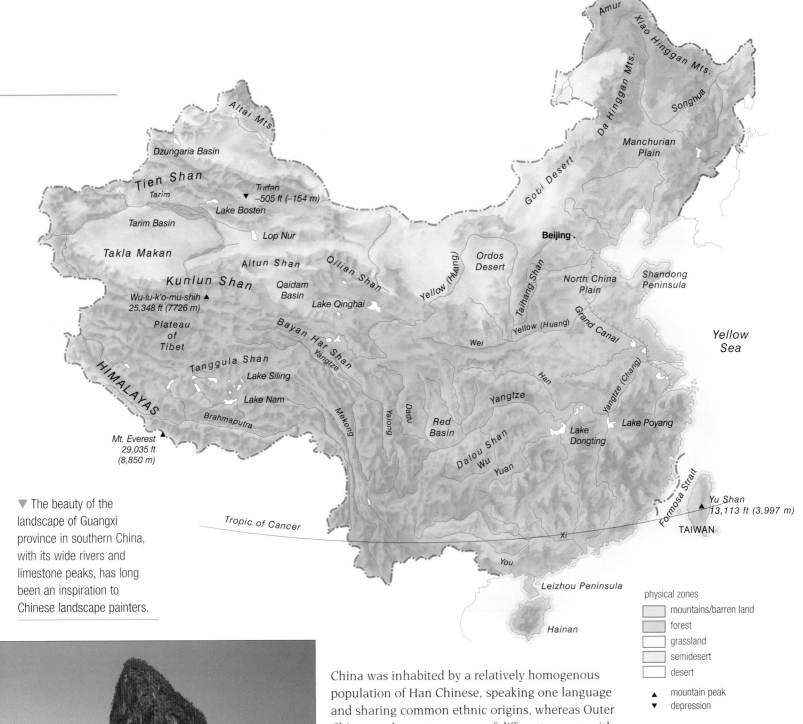

Altai Mts.

Dzungaria Basin

Tien Shan

Tarim

Turfan
▼ −505 ft (−154 m)

Lake Bosten

Tarim Basin

Takla Makan

Altun Shan

Qilian Shan

Ordos
Desert

Gobi Desert

Da Hinggan Mts.

Xiao Hinggan Mts.

Amur

Songhua

Manchurian
Plain

Beijing .

Kunlun Shan

Qaidam
Basin

Lake Qinghai

Taihang Shan

North China
Plain

Shandong
Peninsula

Wu-lu-k'o-mu-shih ▲
25,348 ft (7726 m)

Plateau
of
Tibet

Bayan Har Shan

Yangtze

Yellow (Huang)

Wei

Yellow (Huang)

Grand Canal

Yellow
Sea

Tanggula Shan

Lake Siling

Lake Nam

HIMALAYAS

Brahmaputra

Mekong

Yalong

Dadu

Red
Basin

Yangtze

Han

Yangtze (Chang)

Lake Poyang

Lake
Dongting

Mt. Everest
29,035 ft
(8,850 m)

Dalou Shan
Wu

Yuan

Formosa Strait

Yu Shan
13,113 ft (3,997 m)

TAIWAN

Tropic of Cancer

Xi

You

Leizhou Peninsula

Hainan

physical zones

☐ mountains/barren land
☐ forest
☐ grassland
☐ semidesert
☐ desert

▲ mountain peak
▼ depression

▼ The beauty of the landscape of Guangxi province in southern China, with its wide rivers and limestone peaks, has long been an inspiration to Chinese landscape painters.

China was inhabited by a relatively homogenous population of Han Chinese, speaking one language and sharing common ethnic origins, whereas Outer China was home to a range of different groups with their own languages and cultures.

Outer China has always been a land of extremes. In the south a high plateau gives way to the mountains of Tibet. To the north and east lie the steppelands of Mongolia and Xinjiang, which are well suited for livestock breeding but not for settled agriculture. There rainfall never exceeds 20 inches (50 cm) a year, and winter temperatures can drop as low as −35°F (−37°C).

The steppe was the domain of nomadic herding peoples, long seen by the settled Chinese as a threat. The Great Wall was built to keep them out, but no barrier could permanently exclude them, and the seesawing relationship between the nomads and the settled population would become a constant thread running through China's history.

▲ Map of China's natural features. China is a vast land with diverse physical attributes. To the south and west are huge mountainous ranges and high plateaus, in the north lie large windswept deserts, while the east consists of plains, deltas, and hills.

The Cultivation of Rice

MOST PEOPLE THINK OF RICE AS THE basis of the Chinese diet, but it was not the country's original staple food. The first kingdoms, founded in the north, fed themselves mainly on millet, wheat, and barley. Wild rice did not grow in the loess country of the Yellow (Huang) River basin. Even now rice can be grown there only with difficulty. Rice was not one of the Five Grains that the culture hero Shen Nong gave to humankind in early Chinese mythology (see pages 12–13).

In fact, rice was first domesticated farther south, near the mouth of the Yangtze (Chang) River, probably in the fifth millennium B.C.E. (or earlier). Wild strains flourished naturally in the ideal growing conditions of the delta marshlands. One folktale told how a farmer noticed grasses hanging from a dog's tail as it ran out of the marshes. He inspected the plants and found unfamiliar seeds, which he sowed, thereby cultivating the first crop. To show gratitude, farmers in some parts of China still put out food for dogs at the time of the annual rice harvest.

Whatever its origins, rice cultivation quickly proved its worth. The grains were low in fats but rich in vitamins and minerals (at least when eaten as brown rice, with the bran not removed). Fermented, they made rice wine. Peasant growers wasted nothing. They used the stalks of the plant as thatch for roofing or, plaited, to fashion hats and shoes. The hulls, removed in threshing, were burned for fuel, while the bran went for animal feed. Even broken grains could be used to make flour.

A labor-intensive crop

For all its virtues, rice was not easy to grow. Cultivation was labor intensive, because the plants only gave a high yield if allowed to mature with their roots underwater. That meant that individual shoots had to be transplanted by hand—once they reached a height of about 12 inches (30 cm)—to artificial ponds known as paddies. Harvesting and threshing were also done manually.

More work was required to create the paddies. Typically, farmers enclosed a patch of flat land with a dike of mounded earth and then flooded it to a depth of 2 to 4 inches (5–10 cm) with water from a nearby stream. Once all the riverside lands had been used, they dug irrigation channels to carry water to more distant fields. Finally, when paddies covered the plains, they built terraces on hillsides to provide extra growing space. While most plots were worked by individual families, entire villages collaborated on irrigation and terracing projects, starting a tradition of joint endeavor that had a lasting effect on the farming communities of the south.

Over the centuries much of southeastern China became an intricate patchwork of paddy fields. The reworking of the landscape had political as well as environmental effects. In the troubled times

▼ Rice takes up to 200 days to grow and requires warm, wet conditions. While it is growing, it needs to be flooded either by rain or by irrigation channels. The cultivation of rice is therefore generally restricted to level land and terraces.

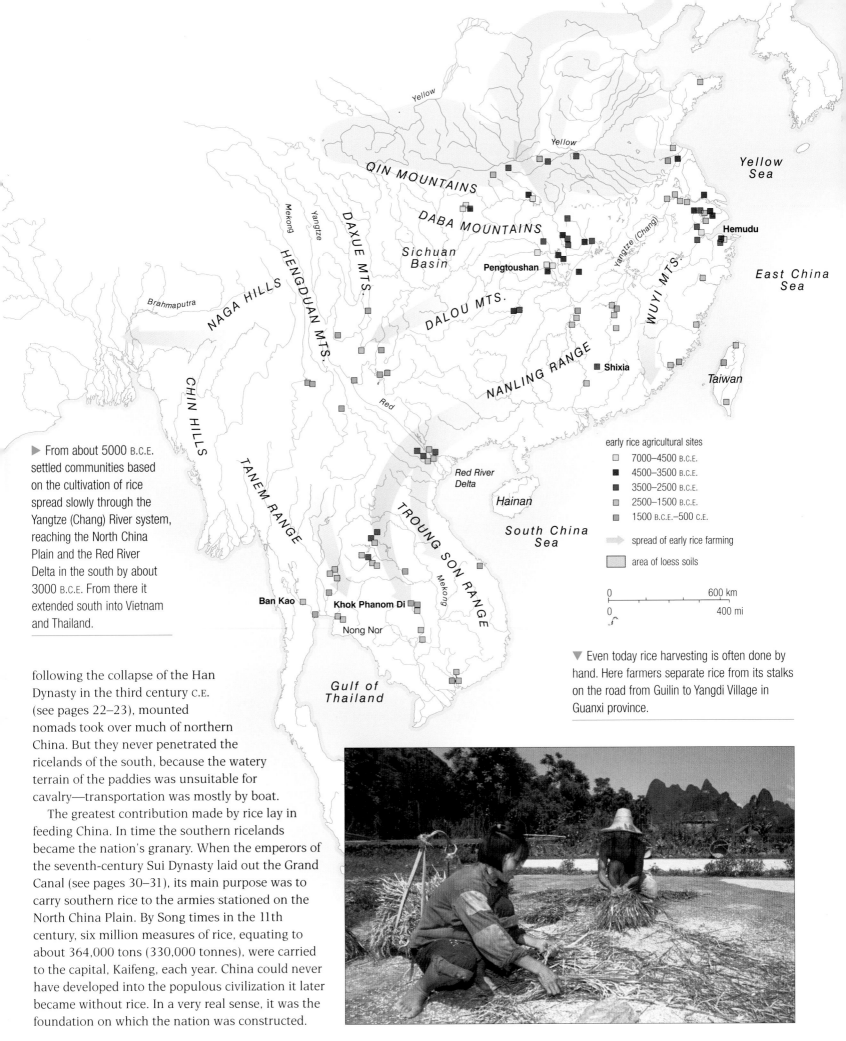

Yellow

Yellow

QIN MOUNTAINS

Yellow
Sea

DABA MOUNTAINS

Hemudu

Sichuan
Basin

East China
Sea

Pengtoushan

DAXUE MTS.

Mekong

Yangtze

Yangtze (Chang)

HENGDUAN MTS.

NAGA HILLS

DALOU MTS.

WUYI MTS.

Brahmaputra

Red

NANLING RANGE

Shixia

Taiwan

CHIN HILLS

early rice agricultural sites

☐ 7000–4500 B.C.E.
■ 4500–3500 B.C.E.
■ 3500–2500 B.C.E.
▨ 2500–1500 B.C.E.
▨ 1500 B.C.E.–500 C.E.

TANEM RANGE

Red River
Delta

Hainan

TROUNG SON RANGE

spread of early rice farming

area of loess soils

▶ From about 5000 B.C.E. settled communities based on the cultivation of rice spread slowly through the Yangtze (Chang) River system, reaching the North China Plain and the Red River Delta in the south by about 3000 B.C.E. From there it extended south into Vietnam and Thailand.

South China
Sea

0   600 km

0   400 mi

Ban Kao

Khok Phanom Di

Mekong

Nong Nor

Gulf of
Thailand

following the collapse of the Han Dynasty in the third century C.E. (see pages 22–23), mounted nomads took over much of northern China. But they never penetrated the ricelands of the south, because the watery terrain of the paddies was unsuitable for cavalry—transportation was mostly by boat.

The greatest contribution made by rice lay in feeding China. In time the southern ricelands became the nation's granary. When the emperors of the seventh-century Sui Dynasty laid out the Grand Canal (see pages 30–31), its main purpose was to carry southern rice to the armies stationed on the North China Plain. By Song times in the 11th century, six million measures of rice, equating to about 364,000 tons (330,000 tonnes), were carried to the capital, Kaifeng, each year. China could never have developed into the populous civilization it later became without rice. In a very real sense, it was the foundation on which the nation was constructed.

▼ Even today rice harvesting is often done by hand. Here farmers separate rice from its stalks on the road from Guilin to Yangdi Village in Guanxi province.

55

Religion and Myth

THE ROOTS OF CHINESE RELIGION STRETCH back into prehistory. Two trends were apparent early on. One was animism, a belief in a world populated by invisible spirits. The other was ancestor worship, part of Chinese culture until recent times.

Ancestor worship was connected with the cult of the extended family, which remains the basis of Chinese society to this day. People looked after not just their existing kinsfolk but also those of previous generations that had passed away. The theory was that the spirits of dead ancestors lived on among the gods in heaven, where they might intercede on behalf of their living relatives if appeased by offerings from the latter. Emperors had a special responsibility to venerate their predecessors. Elaborate mausoleums were built to house the dead rulers' bodies, and ranks of priests conducted rites to honor them. Shang Di, the chief god of early China, was seen as the Supreme Ancestor, so grand that only the current emperor could intercede with him, acting as a go-between for the rest of humankind.

Chinese animism reflected a widespread belief that the natural world was controlled by unseen powers that had to be kept happy if disasters were to be avoided. So there were spirits of the soil and of grain, whose goodwill was needed to ensure fruitful harvests. Powerful beings controlled such forces as the rain and winds. Many geographical features—rivers, lakes, mountains—had guardian spirits that had to be appeased. Emperors made the pilgrimage up Mount Tai, a 5,000-foot (1,500-m) peak in Shandong province, to perform rites on the summit, while for many centuries a beautiful girl was thrown into the Yellow (Huang) River each year to drown. Her spirit was thought to become the river's bride.

Confucius and shamanism

By Confucius's day in the sixth century B.C.E., a new mood of rationalism had developed and such excesses were frowned on. Yet Confucius endorsed the notion of official rites, not through any deep belief in the gods they honored but because they represented respect for tradition and authority. Confucius and his disciples tidied up the early beliefs, turning stories of early culture heroes into legendary history (see pages 12–13) and organizing existing religious practices into a fixed set of rituals.

This practical approach to religion failed to satisfy all Chinese. One tradition in particular did not lend itself to being organized. This was the shamanism practiced by sorcerer–priests called *wu*,

▶ The figure in the drawing is Zhang Boduan, poet and author of *The Inner Teachings of Daoism*. Written in the 11th century, the book describes theories and practices for transforming the mind and refining the self. In ancient times Daoists believed in the existence of supernatural beings (both benevolent and dangerous) and in rituals to maintain a good relationship with these beings.

▶ Pilgrims make the long climb up the "Stairway to Heaven" leading to the Gateway to Heaven Temple at the top of Mount Tai in Shandong province. Mount Tai has been a site of religious worship for more than 3,000 years. Emperors would pay homage to Heaven on the summit and Earth at the foot. It is one of the Daoist "Five Great Mountains" particularly associated with birth and renewal.

who would dance themselves into a frenzy to contact the spirits. The *wu* claimed they could break droughts or produce miracle cures through their privileged position as intermediaries with invisible powers.

Daoism

Something of the instinctive force of the shamans found its way into Daoism (also known as Taoism), a religious-philosophical system that grew up in the Warring States period and still has many followers today. Daoism complemented Confucianism: the latter stood for reason and order, while the Daoist tradition represented all that was intuitive and antirational in Chinese thought and life.

The founding text of Daoism was the *Dao de Jing*, translated as "The Way of Life," said to have been written by Laozi sometime in the Zhou era. The *Dao de Jing* praised nature and solitude over the claims of human society, and emphasized the benefits of *rang* ("yieldingness"). Throughout China's history Confucianism would represent the structured, socially minded aspect of Chinese life, and Daoism would appeal to the mystical and the visionary, providing a continuing source of inspiration for poetry and art.

Medicine and Geomancy

THE ORIGINS OF CHINESE MEDICINE LIE deep in prehistory. The first medical text, the *Neijing*, probably dates from the first century B.C.E., although the knowledge it contained was much older. Tradition ascribed its authorship to the legendary Yellow Emperor himself.

The theory behind traditional medicine involved the concept of *qi*—energy, or the life force—as expressed through its two constituent elements, yin and yang. Yin represented the female principle and was associated with passivity, darkness, and the earth; yang was male and active, linked to light and the heavens. Good health in the Chinese view required a correct balance of yin and yang, which coursed through the body in 12 hypothetical channels. Ill health or even death could result if the channels were blocked.

The great problem with the theory was that it was rarely tested against evidence. Researchers carried out little anatomical work, partly because dissection of corpses was considered disrespectful to the dead. Some criminal cadavers were dissected with imperial approval in the year 16 C.E., but the experiment was not repeated until the Song era nearly a millennium later. The result was that unproven theories about the human body attained the status of dogma. Many

▲ The yin/yang symbol (also known as the Tai Chi symbol) first appeared in Chinese documents nearly 3,000 years ago, and is one of the most recognizable symbols in the world.

of the ideas were affected by numerological considerations, as for instance the notion that the body contained 365 bones and 365 joints, just as the year had 365 days.

In marked contrast, there was also a strong tradition of practical healing that was well ahead of Western practice in many respects. A passage in the *Neijing* suggests that, even in ancient times, Chinese physicians understood that blood circulates around the body. They were also inoculating people against smallpox well over 1,000 years before the practice became familiar in the West. Surgery was being performed by the second century C.E., although its greatest practitioner, Hua Tuo, was accused of attempted assassination and died under torture after proposing brain surgery for an emperor who had recurrent headaches.

Herbal remedies

Chinese doctors could draw on an extensive knowledge of herbal and other medicines. In the 16th century C.E. a physician named Li Shizhen collated more than 1,000 existing medicinal treatises to produce the *Great Pharmacopoeia*. It included 2,000 separate drugs and 8,000 prescriptions. Substances used in China long before their benefits were known

▶ An acupuncture chart dating from the Ming Dynasty. This detailed anatomical print shows the paths by which vital energy flows around the body and indicates points for the application of needles.

◀ A Chinese herbalist's cabinet holds a range of traditional medicines that are used to provide cures for various ailments, including allergies, skin disease, and digestive complaints.

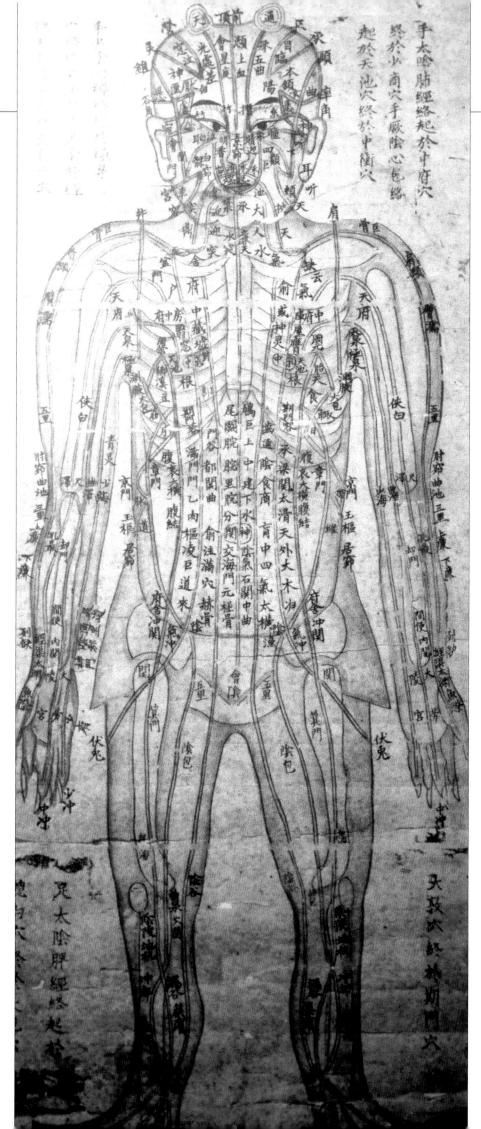

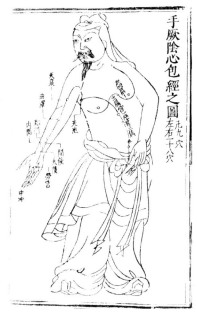

▶ A Chinese anatomy drawing made in 1031 by Trong Jin Tchou, showing acupuncture points on the arm.

in the West included iron (to treat anemia), iodine, aconite, kaolin, camphor, and *Cannabis sativa* (Indian hemp), which was mixed with wine and used as an anesthetic. Chinese physicians also prescribed the herb *mahuang*, now used in asthma drugs.

Acupuncture

Acupuncture (the practice of inserting needles into the skin to therapeutic effect) had an equally ancient pedigree—a section of the *Neijing* was devoted to the subject. The treatment was often combined with moxibustion (burning mounds of the dried moxa plant with the heated end away from the skin, which felt only the associated warmth). Acupuncture was closely linked to the yin and yang theory of health. The points where the acupuncture needles were inserted were supposedly located on the 12 channels, or meridians, carrying *qi* around the body. A treatise dating from the third century C.E. already listed 349 separate acupuncture points, while by the eighth century there were exams for trainee practitioners.

Geomancy

The theory of the flow of *qi* was extended beyond the realm of medicine by Daoist geomancers (diviners), who claimed to be able to identify its passage through the landscape just as physicians did in the body. The siting of buildings and of graves could affect its free movement, supposedly bringing good or bad luck. The technique of steering the flow so that *qi* was channeled but not obstructed became known as feng shui ("wind and water," two of the elements involved). It is largely dismissed by modern science, yet continues to be practiced.

Confucius and Confucianism

CHINA'S MOST INFLUENTIAL THINKER, Confucius, was born in 551 B.C.E. during the Warring States period, when China was divided into many rival kingdoms. The ruling Zhou Dynasty exerted only nominal authority over unruly vassal kings, who in practice went their own way. During this time there was an upsurge in intellectual activity that saw the so-called 100 Schools of philosophy bloom, each with its own particular solution to the problems of the day.

Confucius—in Chinese Kongfuzi, or "Kong the Master"—grew up in the eastern state of Lu. He was born into an impoverished aristocratic family, and in adult life he fitted naturally into the class of *shi*, or gentleman-scholars. His father died before Confucius was born, and the infant philosopher was raised by his mother. He started his career as an administrator in the service of the Lu royal house, initially managing the royal stables and keeping the accounts for a state-owned granary.

◄ An illustration of Confucius (551–479 B.C.E.) from a rubbing of a marble slab in a Confucian temple. Confucius's thoughts and writings were developed into a system of philosophy known as Confucianism.

Eventually he gave up his job to pursue a wandering life as a teacher, helping train the children of the elite for positions of responsibility. As his reputation spread, rulers consulted him on political matters, but he never seems to have found one willing to follow his precepts to the full. By the time of his death, he had attracted a loyal band of followers. Although he left no writings that have survived, his disciples compiled a collection of his sayings, the *Analects*, that preserved his message for the centuries to come.

Confucius's vision was a deeply conservative one. Living in troubled times, he dreamed of a past golden age when China had been united under the rule of virtuous emperors. He accepted the idea of a social hierarchy and he believed that order could only be achieved if everyone accepted their own place. "Let the ruler be a ruler and the minister a minister," he said. "Let the father be a father and the son a son."

Self-discipline and respect

Much of Confucius's thought revolved around the notion of *li*. Usually translated as "propriety," this Chinese term also implies a respect for moral and social obligations, whether through courtesy and etiquette or by the correct performance of the rites that made up a large part of traditional Chinese religion. Unusually, Confucius was more concerned with the rituals as a socially cohesive force than with the gods they addressed. "I stand in awe of the spirits," he replied when asked about his religious beliefs, "but keep them at a distance."

In family life, the sage expected children to show respect for their parents and for their departed ancestors. Politically, subjects were to show similar obedience to those in authority over them, since the state in the Confucian view was simply the family writ large, with the ruler presiding over it as a patriarchal father presides over his household. Yet kings had moral obligations too. They had to practice self-discipline and study widely so as to develop the generosity of spirit needed to reign justly. Confucius's advice to rulers was: "Approach your duties with

Sayings of Confucius

Confucius's sayings from the *Analects* provided guidance on the exercise of wisdom, virtue, friendship, and work, among other subjects.

"To know is to know that you know nothing. That is the meaning of true knowledge."

"He who wishes to secure the good of others has already secured his own."

"Our greatest glory is not in never falling but in rising every time we fall."

"The perfecting of one's self is the fundamental base of all progress and all moral development."

"Everyone eats and drinks, yet only a few appreciate the taste of food."

"Everything has its beauty, but not everyone sees it."

"Choose a job you love, and you will never have to work a day in your life."

"People with virtue must speak out; people who speak are not all virtuous."

"Do not be concerned about others not appreciating you. Be concerned about your not appreciating others."

"Have no friends not equal to yourself."

reverence and be trustworthy in what you say; avoid excessive expenditure and love your fellow men, employ the labor of the common people only in the appropriate seasons."

Confucius's doctrine was ideally suited to serve as a state ideology, emphasizing as it did the responsibilities of both ruler and ruled. In later centuries it would become official doctrine in China, learned by all would-be bureaucrats, who repeated its lessons in exams for government posts. Yet there was another aspect to the sage's thought that helped explain its enduring appeal for individuals as well as for officials. This was the guidance he gave on personal morality, extolling the value of the "superior man" who, through wisdom and control of the emotions, trains himself to be upright, tolerant, and above all humane. The model that Confucius proposed was difficult to attain, yet it proved an inspiration for countless generations.

◀ Confucius inspired many scholars during and after his lifetime. Here Zilu, a disciple of Confucius, studies as he walks by the light of the moon. He died in 480 B.C.E. while attempting to protect the prince he served.

▼ Confucius traveled to many states in China to give advice to rulers. His preferred method of travel was the ox cart, which appears in a number of representations of the philosopher, including this 19th-century illustration from *The Life of Confucius*.

The Underground Army

IN 1974 MEMBERS OF A FARMING COMMUNE digging a well east of Xian in Shanxi province made an exciting discovery. About 13 feet (4 m) down, their shovels struck pieces of terra-cotta (fired clay). On inspection, they proved to be fragments of life-size statues of soldiers in ancient dress. The farmers contacted the authorities, because they knew the discovery was probably significant. The site was less than a mile (1,200 m) east of one of China's most important historical monuments, a mound covering the tomb of the First Emperor, Shi Huangdi.

The emperor's tomb

Because of the Chinese tradition of respect for the dead, archaeologists had left the tomb intact, but much was known about it from ancient literary sources. More than 700,000 workers were said to have labored on its construction. The underground realm they created was a miniature replica of Shi Huangdi's empire, complete with liquid-mercury versions of the Yellow (Huang) and Yangtze (Chang) Rivers endlessly flowing to an imitation sea. The roof of the tomb was said to be studded with precious stones simulating the constellations of the night sky. Beneath them, models of palaces and pavilions surrounded the brass tomb in which the body of the emperor was laid. To secure the complex against robbers, crossbows were positioned with the strings drawn, ready to fire their bolts at intruders. Many of the laborers working on the site were reportedly buried alive inside when it was sealed up, the better to protect its secrets.

Much of this account might not have been believed were it not for the fact that the First Emperor was known to have had an enduring fascination with death and immortality. Ancient historians described how, in his later years, he paid Daoist magicians to produce an elixir of life. Even more bizarrely, he dispatched a fleet of ships with 3,000 young people aboard to seek out three islands of the immortals said to exist somewhere in the China Sea. No more was ever heard of the crew, although legends later claimed they settled in Japan.

Terra-cotta warriors

Archaeologists were excited by the figures the diggers had found, even though at first they could not understand what they were doing so far beyond the mausoleum's outer perimeter. The answer was provided by a massive excavation project still not completed to this day. The diggers found a huge pit

▲ The largest excavation pit contains thousands of terra-cotta soldiers in battle formation. Eleven columns of footsoldiers follow rows of crossbowmen.

▲ Among the ranks of soldiers are many horses, used for pulling wooden chariots as well as for carrying riders.

some 760 feet (230 m) long by 200 feet (60 m) wide. Ten earth ramps divided it into separate corridors, each one containing columns of life-size terra-cotta foot-soldiers, protected by a vanguard of charioteers and crossbowmen. The pit contained in excess of 6,000 figures, most of which had been shattered when the roof caved in sometime in antiquity, and which restorers painstakingly pieced together.

Later investigations revealed three smaller pits alongside the first one. The second contained more than 1,400 charioteers and cavalrymen with their mounts. The third was much smaller, and is thought to have represented a headquarters for the army command. The fourth pit was empty, suggesting that work was not completed at the time of the First Emperor's death in 210 B.C.E.

Dozens of other pits have since been found closer to the mausoleum. Some contained models of dancers and acrobats to entertain the emperor in the afterlife. Others had statues of birds. One contained two half-size models of the emperor's chariot, with bronze horses still in harness. The emperor's tomb itself remains unexcavated, guarding its secrets, but tests with probes have confirmed the presence of mercury vapor inside. Enough has been found, though, to indicate that the whole area around the tomb—25 square miles (66 sq. km)—was one vast necropolis designed to provide the dead ruler with all the facilities he enjoyed while he was alive.

▲ The headdresses and hairstyles of the figures vary according to regiment and rank. Cavalrymen wore close-fitting caps, but infantrymen had their hair wound into elaborate topknots.

◄ The figures, each with a distinctive face, are thought to be likenesses of real soldiers. The lower part of each body is solid, while the upper part is hollow. The figures were originally painted in bright colors that have now faded.

Calligraphy

CALLIGRAPHY, THE TECHNIQUE OF beautiful writing, is one of the most admired art forms in China. Combining the skills of painting and the written word, it has no real Western equivalent. Writing developed independently in China, as it did in Mesopotamia, Egypt, and (later) America. The first written characters took the form of symbols carved by diviners on animal bones, which were used to predict future events. Markings of this kind found in Henan province have been dated to as far back as 6000 B.C.E. (see pages 14–15).

These early inscriptions were simple pictograms, used as memory aids to record the diviners' findings. Another 4,000 years would go by before the script known today developed, combining pictographic elements with abstract symbols. The only writings to have survived from Shang and Zhou times were still inscriptions, on bronze vessels by that time as well as on oracle bones. The characters themselves were angular, since they were formed by using a stylus (a pen-shaped stick made of hard wood or bone), the only available writing implement.

The revolution that made calligraphy possible came with the introduction of writing brushes sometime around the year 300 B.C.E. (A later, unreliable tradition would ascribe their first use to Meng Tian, the general commissioned by the First Emperor to build the Great Wall.) With the brushes, which were tipped at first with deer's hair and later with rabbit fur, scribes could make ink markings on flat surfaces. The first books took the form of characters written in columns on slats of wood or bamboo, bound together with thread. Some works intended for the emperor and other wealthy individuals were inscribed on rolls of silk.

Development of paper

Paper was first made not long after the brush and ink were introduced—a fragment made from hemp has been dated to about 100 B.C.E. Initially it was made by pounding fibrous material to a pulp and coating the dried sediment with gelatin. The resulting material was rough-textured and was used only for wrapping. The earliest examples of paper used for writing date from the start of the first millennium C.E.

Composed of separate characters each representing an entire word, Chinese script lent itself naturally to a visual, individualistic style of writing. Calligraphers and painters used the

▲ Ancient Chinese diviners used animal bones, known as oracle bones, to record their activities. These characters carved on an oracle bone date from about 1000 B.C.E. (Shang Dynasty).

▼ The craft of papermaking has changed little since it was invented in about 100 B.C.E. First, vegetable material such as leaves, mulberry bark, and bamboo shoots (A) were pulped with water in a trough. Next the pulp was spread onto a fine screen or mesh (B). Finally, the water drained away to leave a criss-cross of matted fibers that dried to form a sheet of paper (C).

same brushes and ink, so the two arts were always closely allied. Many painters also practiced calligraphy, while some individuals such as Su Shi, one of the great talents of the Song era, were accomplished poets as well. The result was an intermingling of the literary and artistic traditions that had no equivalent in Western culture.

Calligraphy as art

Calligraphy first came into its own as an art form in the Six Dynasties period that followed the collapse of the Han Empire (see pages 22–23). Northern aristocrats, fleeing barbarian incursions to settle in southern China, brought the tradition of the scholar-artist to their new home.

The greatest practitioner of the time was Wang Xizhi, who would become revered as the "sage of calligraphy." He and his successors established the art's reputation as an occupation for the leisured class, who alone had the time and training to develop the necessary skills. The literary bent of the classic calligraphers was reflected in the texts they chose to copy—usually poems or extracts from the Confucian classics.

Different styles of brushwork developed over the centuries. In the Song and Yuan eras it was common to combine words and pictures in the same work. Calligraphy is still practiced today, and is considered the most sublime form of art in Chinese culture.

A

B

C
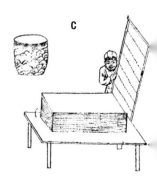

▼ The character *yong*, meaning "eternity," combines the eight basic strokes used in Chinese calligraphy. Although there are many more than these basic elements, the excellence of all calligraphy is largely determined by the individual brush marks.

▶ The earliest system of writing used pictures (pictograms) to represent objects. Over the centuries, pictures were simplified and new symbols developed, as seen here in the characters for *wàn,* or "scorpion" (top row) and *yáng,* or "sheep" (bottom row).

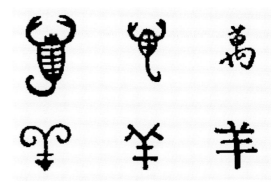

▶ Chinese writing has evolved through a number of different types of "scripts." Right: This example of Seal script was used on a Zhou Dynasty bronze vessel. Center: An example of *caoshu* (Grass script). This rubbing is taken from an engraving of the work of Wang Xizhi (fourth century C.E.), with whom this style is associated. Strokes could be joined together and several characters written with one continuous flow of the brush, often making it hard to read. Far right: *Kaishu* (Standard or Regular script) derived from *lishu* (official or clerical script) and developed in the first century C.E. It is still in use today. The strokes are clearly defined and are more upright and angular.

Painting and Sculpture

THE BEGINNINGS OF CHINESE PAINTING ARE lost in the mists of time. The earliest surviving fragments date from the Han era and already show a sure and distinctive touch. The continuous history of the art can be traced from the fourth century C.E. It reached a peak in the Tang and Song eras and by Ming times was showing signs of decline, marked partly by a tendency to decoration and an exaggerated respect for the traditions of the past.

Chinese traditions

Chinese painters used the same materials as calligraphers (see pages 64–65), namely brushes and ink, supplemented in their case by color pigments, which they tended to apply sparingly. There was a persistent tradition in Chinese art of monochrome works, painted in dark ink on a white ground. Ink could not be erased or easily painted over once the brush had touched the painting's surface, so its use favored spontaneity and quick brushstrokes.

Chinese painters only began to use the canvases familiar in Western art in modern times. Previously, their favorite medium was the scroll, which could be rolled up and put away when not in use. Vertical hanging scrolls, 2 to 6 feet (0.6–1.8 m) long, were the main form of wall decoration in many homes. Hand-scrolls, in contrast, unrolled horizontally, and were used for panoramic landscapes. Rarely much more than 1 foot (30 cm) wide, they could be anything up to 30 feet (9 m) in length. Viewers usually opened them in sections, revealing a newspaper-width span at a time, so they could be used to show the different stages of a journey or a tour of an entire garden or city. Painters in Tang and Song times also sketched smaller scenes on the backs of fans or in albums reminiscent of Western artists' sketchbooks.

Chinese painting grew up with close ties to calligraphy, to the extent that many artists chose to include poems or other inscriptions in their works. As a result, a tradition of poet-painters developed from the Tang era on. One result in a land that revered literary scholarship was to boost the prestige of artists at a time when their Western counterparts were regarded as little more than skilled artisans.

▶ Standing guard outside the Imperial Palace, Beijing, is this impressive bronze lion. The palace was built by the Ming royal family but is now China's largest national museum, housing about one million valuable works of art.

▼ An eighth-century copy of a section of a handscroll painting attributed to Gu Kaizhi (c.345–406), entitled *The Admonitions of the Instructress to the Court Ladies*. This scene shows a virtuous concubine intercepting a black bear about to attack the emperor.

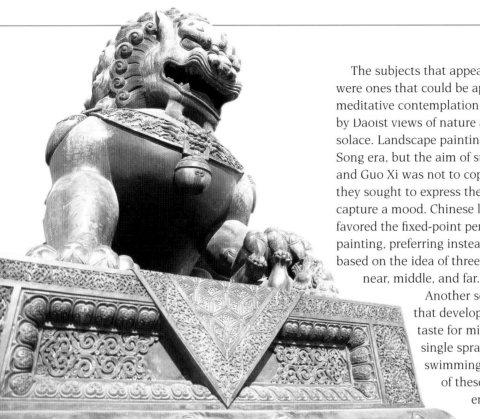

The subjects that appealed to the scholar painters were ones that could be approached in a spirit of meditative contemplation. Many were influenced by Daoist views of nature as a source of spiritual solace. Landscape painting came into its own in the Song era, but the aim of such masters as Ma Yuan and Guo Xi was not to copy views from life. Instead, they sought to express the essence of a scene or to capture a mood. Chinese landscape artists never favored the fixed-point perspective of Western painting, preferring instead a shifting viewpoint based on the idea of three separate distances: near, middle, and far.

Another school of Chinese painting that developed from the Song era had a taste for minimalist subject matter: a single spray of bamboo, or three fish swimming. In their own way, the best of these works have as much energy as the bustling city panoramas that were also popular at the time.

▼ For centuries Chinese artists have drawn inspiration from nature. This 18th-century painting by Li Shan is entitled *Narcissus, Bamboo, and Rocks*.

Tomb sculptures

Early Chinese sculpture is known mainly from tombs. Archaeologists have discovered bronze works of astonishing quality, notably a figure of a horse with one hoof resting on a swallow's back, dating to the second century C.E. The arrival of Buddhism (see pages 68–69) was a huge influence on statuary and painting. Thousands of carvings and wall paintings found in caves along the routes that brought the new religion to China rank among the nation's greatest artistic treasures. Indian and central Asian influences predominated at first, but from the sixth century on a national style developed. Its masterpieces included startlingly realistic seated portraits of bodhisattvas and *lohans*—the Buddhist equivalents of saints.

▼ The Sacred Way leading to the tombs of the Ming emperors near Beijing is lined with marble figures sculpted from whole stones. The elephant represented the vastness of the territory controlled by the Ming court. Note how its back legs bend the wrong way—the sculptor had evidently never seen a real elephant.

The Spread of Buddhism

ORIGINATING IN INDIA IN ABOUT 500 B.C.E., Buddhism was first introduced to China in the first century C.E. by merchants traveling along the Silk Road. The earliest surviving reference dates from 65 C.E., when the Han emperor Ming Di said of a nephew that he "recites the subtle words of Huang-Lao and respectfully performs the gentle sacrifices of the Buddha." The words are significant, because Huang-Lao was a Daoist god, and at first Buddhism was regarded by most native Chinese as a Daoist sect (see pages 56–57). Over the centuries the two religions were to influence one another strongly.

At first the new faith made little headway in a land that already had its own gods as well as the rational creed of Confucianism (see pages 60–61). Buddhism was viewed with suspicion as a foreign import, while its taste for metaphysical speculation ran against the pragmatic Chinese concern for the here and now. (Metaphysics is a branch of philosophy concerned with explaining the world.) In addition, Buddhist monks were vowed to celibacy, a tradition that ran counter to the Confucian emphasis on family life.

Buddhism accepted

The situation changed radically in the confusion of the Six Dynasties period (see pages 28–29), when traditional Chinese culture was challenged as never before and people were forced to look inward for salvation. Buddhist doctrines spread rapidly in northern China, whose so-called barbarian rulers felt no hostility to the new faith. Ordinary people flocked to Buddhist fortress–monasteries as places of safety when danger threatened. The Northern Wei Dynasty established by the Tuoba people was especially accepting of the faith, promoting it almost as a state religion. By the late fifth century, nine-tenths of northern China's population was said to be Buddhist.

The situation was different in southern China. Here Buddhism was fashionable first in intellectual circles and only gradually spread to the population at large. It established a firm foothold at the Eastern Jin court; by the time the dynasty ended in 420, there were 1,768 monasteries and 24,000 monks and nuns.

In later years Buddhism found a fresh champion in Emperor Wu, founder of the Liang, one of the Eastern Jin's short-lived successor dynasties. A fervent Buddhist, he sponsored the construction of temples, forbade the use of animals for medicinal or sacrificial purposes, and on at least two occasions was persuaded only with difficulty from abdicating to become a monk himself.

In the early days Chinese Buddhists had little access to the texts on which their religion was based. That situation changed thanks to the efforts of intrepid monks who made epic journeys to India in search of the holy scriptures. The best-known, Faxian, was already over 60 years old when he set off overland through Afghanistan and the Hindu Kush mountains in 399. He returned 14 years later, having spent more than a year on the sea journey back, carefully guarding the manuscripts he had copied.

Translation of Indian texts

The Indian texts needed translating from Sanskrit, and no one did more to advance this work than Kumarajiva. A good-humored missionary from central Asia, he spent 20 years in captivity in northern China before being placed in charge of a team of scholar-monks in the old Han capital of Changan. Between them they produced Chinese versions of 98 separate scriptures, 52 of which survive to this day.

The school of Buddhism that took root in China was the Mahayana ("Great Vehicle") version also

▶ Outstanding examples of Chinese Buddhist cave art from the fifth and sixth centuries can be found in the Yungang Grottoes outside Datong city, Shanxi province. The cave containing this sculpted Buddha is richly painted and carved on every surface.

▼ Buddhism began to spread into China during the first century C.E. The chief route by which it traveled was from northern India and Kashmir via the Buddhist kingdoms of central Asia (such as Khotan and Kucha) and the Silk Roads that came down the Gansu corridor to Changan.

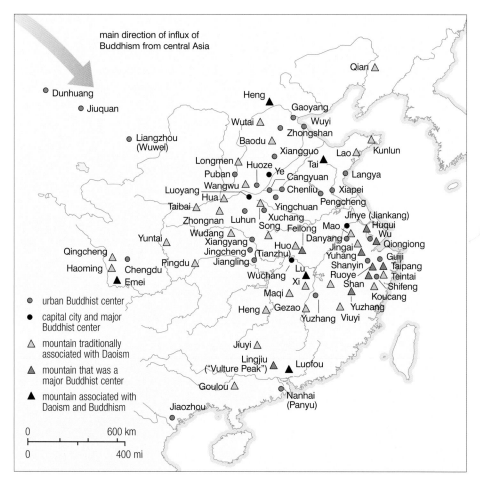

main direction of influx of Buddhism from central Asia

Qian △

Dunhuang
Jiuquan
Heng ▲
Gaoyang
Wutai △
Wuyi
Zhongshan
Liangzhou (Wuwei)
Baodu △
Xiangguo
Lao △
Kunlun
Longmen △
Huoze
Tai ▲
Puban △
Ye
Cangyuan
Langya
Wangwu △
Chenliu
Xiapei
Luoyang
Hua △
Pengcheng
Taibai △
Yingchuan
Jinye (Jiankang)
Zhongnan
Luhun
Xuchang
Mao △
Huqui
Song Feilong
Wu
Wudang △
Danyang
Qiongiong
Yuntai △
Xiangyang
Huo △
Jingai
Jingcheng (Tianzhu)
Yuhang
Guiji
Qingcheng
Jiangling
Lu
Shanyin
Taipang
Haoming △
Pingdu △
Wuchang
Ruoye
Teintai
Chengdu
Xi △
Shan △
Shifeng
Emei ▲
Maqi △
Koucang
Heng △
Gezao △
Yuzhang
Yuzhang
Viuyi
Jiuyi △
Lingjiu ("Vulture Peak")
Luofou
Goulou △
Nanhai (Panyu)
Jiaozhou

● urban Buddhist center
● capital city and major Buddhist center
△ mountain traditionally associated with Daoism
▲ mountain that was a major Buddhist center
▲ mountain associated with Daoism and Buddhism

0   600 km
0   400 mi

▲ Drawings showing the changing representations of the Buddha over time:
1. c.460–80; 2. c.495–530; 3. c.550–80; 4. c.580–620; 5. 620–750.

adopted in Tibet, Nepal, Mongolia, Korea, and Japan. Encouraging popular veneration of bodhisattvas—saintly individuals who have delayed their own salvation to aid humankind—it emphasized compassion over the contemplative rigor of the Buddha's original faith.

In time it became firmly entrenched in the nation's culture, joining Confucianism and Daoism as one of three belief systems that have helped shape Chinese thought over the centuries. Like Daoism, Buddhism had a particular influence on the arts: the many thousands of sculptures decorating cave complexes at Yungang and at Longmen, south of Luoyang, are among the enduring masterpieces of the nation's cultural heritage.

▶ The main Buddha Lushena (meaning "illumination") and his bodhisattvas in the Fengxian Temple at the Longmen Grottoes in Luoyang, Henan province. Work was begun on this enormous sculpture in 672 and was completed four years later.

Bureaucracy and Government

T HE ROOTS OF CHINESE BUREAUCRACY GO back at least as far as the First Emperor, if not earlier. By the year 220 B.C.E. China already had provinces that were governed by imperial appointees, a prime minister, a cabinet made up of ministers responsible for major areas of government, and even an official known as the "grandee secretary" whose job was to oversee the efficiency of the rest of the administration.

The principle of attracting individuals of talent and merit into government, whatever their social background, also developed early in Chinese history. There were obvious advantages for the emperors in appointing high officers of state from beyond the ranks of the great nobles. After all, individuals who owed their advancement to imperial favor alone were less likely to set themselves up as rivals for supreme power.

So the custom of choosing future administrators by examination gradually developed. Its origins lay in the Han practice of seeking out promising candidates in the provinces and sending them to the capital for training (see pages 24–25). It was only under the Tang and Song emperors, though, that the system was fully developed.

Provincial training grounds

By Song times publicly funded schools were established in the provinces to train students for the government exams. Many were housed in converted Buddhist temples and were supported by small estates that provided revenue for their upkeep. Pupils first had to acquire basic literacy skills before going on to study the Confucian classics. The most prestigious course of study involved poetry composition as well as writing essays on policy matters and the Confucian system of laws.

Only a tiny minority—1 percent or less—of those who took the prefectural exams went on to the next stage, which was held in the Song capital of Kaifeng and supervised by government officials. This test weeded out another 90 percent or more of the entrants, leaving just a handful of hopefuls to face the third and final round of examinations, which were conducted in the presence of the emperor himself. Only about 200 palace degrees were awarded each year, graded "Passed with distinction," "Formally qualified," or simply "Passed." Successful candidates were by that time mostly in their late 20s or early 30s, and were ready to take up lucrative positions in the imperial administration.

The exam system was never entirely based on merit. People from a peasant background generally had neither the time nor the resources to attain the level of literacy that was needed to gain a foothold on the ladder. In addition, locally prominent families were able to use their influence to get their children into the schools that prepared pupils for selection.

Even so, the tests succeeded in broadening the pool of talent from which the governing class was drawn. One modern estimate suggests that by the 11th century 40 percent of the nation's leading officials sprang from obscure families. The system also ensured that aristocratic students who obtained administrative posts had to work for their positions, gaining them at least partly through merit rather than by an accident of birth.

The bureaucracy took its guiding ethos from the works of Confucius. Its best employees accepted the dictum of the 11th-century reformer, Fan Zhongyan, that "the true scholar should be the first to become anxious about the world's troubles and the last to enjoy its happiness."

Bureaucracy in practice

Yet only a handful of top government officials ever got the chance to put the ideals they had acquired into practice for the benefit of the nation as a whole. The day-to-day reality of life within the bureaucracy was normally much more mundane. Generations of overworked government officials would probably have recognized the description that a Han poet gave of the daily round:

> "Office work, a wearisome jumble;
> Ink drafts, a crosshatch of deletions and smears;
> Racing the writing brush, no time to eat,
> Sun slanting down but never a break;
> Swamped and muddled in records and reports,
> Head spinning until it's senseless and numb."

Even so, such drudgery helped hold the Chinese empire together. The work of the bureaucrats was a shaping feature of Chinese civilization for more than 2,000 years.

◀ This 19th-century engraving depicts the emperor of Cochin China (now Vietnam) and his ministers. Since the days of the Qin, emperors ruled with the assistance of bureaucrats. The Qin designed a system based on two levels of government—commanderies and prefectures. The later Han Dynasty added provinces at the top, creating three tiers of administration.

Poetry

CHINA HAS THE LONGEST UNINTERRUPTED poetic tradition in the world. The earliest work was collected in the *Shi Jing* (Book of Odes), one of the five classic texts that make up the Confucian canon of early Chinese literature. A long-lasting tradition claims that Confucius himself edited this anthology of work from the Shang and Zhou eras, which contains 305 separate poems, classified either as popular ballads, courtly songs, or eulogies. As the English title suggests, the poems were originally composed as lyrics intended to be accompanied by music, and in some cases by dancing as well. The link with music has survived into modern times, and even today people reading Chinese poetry aloud tend to chant the verses rather than just speak them.

Subsequently poetry developed as an art of the educated classes, written in a literary style that did not reflect everyday speech. For the most part China's poets belonged to the class of scholar-functionaries, and some reached high ranks in government service—one of the greatest, Bai Juyi, ended his career as the governor of Suzhou province.

Such men were immersed in the Confucian classics from an early age. Yet Daoism was an equally strong influence, and the Daoist ideal of the wise hermit contemplating nature from a secluded retreat high in the mountains or deep in the forest had a lasting place in the Chinese imagination. There was also a continuing folk tradition of ballads.

The wandering poet

Chinese poetry reached a peak under the Tang Dynasty. Works by more than 2,000 individuals have survived, and among them are some of the nation's greatest writers. Every Chinese child grows up knowing the story of Li Bo, a scholar and a bohemian who spent his life wandering across China and socializing with friends in literary groups known as the "Seven Idlers of the Bamboo Grove" (an affectionate parody of the Daoist "Seven Sages of the Bamboo Grove") and the "Eight Immortals of the Wine Cup."

Invited to court, Li Bo enjoyed three years of imperial favor before being expelled, supposedly for offending the Chief Eunuch while inebriated at a

▶ Jiangyou in Sichuan province is said to have been the childhood home of the ancient "wandering" poet Li Bo. His house is in the center of the photograph. In the background are the famous twin peaks of Mount Doutuan.

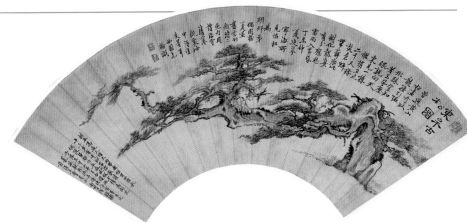

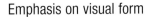

▲ Chinese visual art and poetry have always gone hand in hand. This Qing Dynasty fan is decorated with a painting of an unusual pine tree. The inscription at the top states that it was painted for the artist's brother, while the poem on the left-hand side describes the pine branch—it was 13 paces long and flowers sprouted there from seeds brought by the wind.

◀ A painting from the mid-12th century, illustrating the Odes of Chen, part of the *Shi Jing* (Book of Odes), a collection of poems and folk songs said to have been compiled by Confucius. The poems are personal expressions on themes such as courtship, marriage, work, and loss.

state banquet. He was later exiled to a remote part of western China, but took so long on the way, stopping off constantly to stay with friends, that he still had not arrived three years later when a general amnesty was granted. Legend has it that he eventually died while drunk, trying to embrace the moon's reflection in a river. (The story recalls the fate of Qu Yuan, an earlier master who drowned himself in the Milo River, a tragedy commemorated each year in the Dragon Boat festivals held across the Chinese world—see pages 90–91.)

Emphasis on visual form

One distinctive characteristic of Chinese poetry is its visual quality. From early times the poet's art has been closely linked to calligraphy (see pages 64–65), and the best works have always looked, as well as sounded, beautiful. Even today many Chinese families have poems in addition to paintings decorating the walls of their homes.

The nature of Chinese characters, which has shaped the look of Chinese poems, has also left its mark on their content. Their largely monosyllabic quality lends itself to terse expression, and most works are short, aiming to capture a moment or a mood in just a few lines. Long narrative or epic poems are mostly noticeable by their absence. The economy of classic Chinese poetry, which prefers concrete symbols to metaphors and seeks to cut out unnecessary words, appeals to modern Western tastes. In the 20th century it had a significant impact on the development of American poetry.

By the Ming era the poetic tradition had lost a little of its freshness. Poetry too often became an academic exercise designed to show off scholars' skills in handling words. Yet the art continues to command great prestige. Even the Communist leader Mao Zedong liked it to be known that he wrote poems while fighting the civil war that led to the creation of the People's Republic of China in 1949.

Architecture

FOR AN ANCIENT CIVILIZATION, CHINA HAS surprisingly few very old buildings. Little has survived that predates the Ming, since most earlier structures were made of perishable wood.

Town planning

Even so, historians know much about early Chinese architecture from literary sources and archaeological evidence, notably small clay models and sculptures found in Han tombs. They have seen that from early on the nation's rulers seem to have encouraged town planning, partly for defense. Most cities were laid out on a rectangular plan, surrounded by massive walls to protect the communities within. The same writing symbol was used for "city" and "wall." These fortifications were often immense. Even 3,500 years ago the city of Zhengzhou was protected by a wall that stretched for 4 miles (7 km). By Ming times the Nanjing city wall was 20 miles (32 km) long and 60 feet (18 m) high.

Inside the walls, the cities were typically laid out on a north–south axis, with two main avenues meeting at right angles in the city center. Sometimes the junction was guarded by a drum tower, where guards were stationed to keep order and a drum sounded to mark the hours of the day. There were four apertures in the tower at ground level and four gates in the outside wall, one for each thoroughfare.

Houses, too, were oriented to north and south, with the living quarters facing south. Archaeological evidence suggests that the basic pattern of housing changed little until recent times. Homes were built around courtyards—a single cramped quadrangle if the owner was poor, but a whole series of courts and gardens for the wealthy, housing several generations of an extended family. The yards were flanked by detached halls subdivided into smaller rooms.

Distinctive curved roofs

Temples and palaces mostly repeated the same courtyard layout on a grander scale. Among their most distinctive features were curving roofs with overhanging eaves. The roofs owed their flexible design to construction methods that differed from those of the West. In China a building's roof was normally put up before the walls. It was supported on purlins (horizontal beams) and crossbeams resting on columns rather than on triangular roof tresses. The walls, made of wooden panels or brick, were filled in later and were not load-bearing to any large extent. This system gave Chinese architects freedom to vary the silhouette of their buildings.

▼ The typical upcurved design of Chinese roofs had symbolic significance as well as structural practicality. They protected the inhabitants not only from the elements but also from evil spirits, which were believed to travel in straight lines.

Over the centuries different regional styles came to the fore. Southerners generally favored sharply curved roofs with upward-tilting eaves, decorated with figures representing mythological creatures and Daoist gods. Northern tastes were on the whole more restrained, with gentle curves and ornamentation that was restricted to the corner ridges.

The strongest foreign influences on Chinese architecture came with the arrival of Buddhism from India (see pages 68–69). The cave temples of western China, for example, are strongly marked by the styles of the subcontinent. In the Chinese heartland, however, Buddhist places of worship were hardly distinguishable from Confucian and Daoist shrines, except that many were adorned with pagodas. These multistoried towers may initially have been modelled on stupas—domed edifices housing Buddhist relics that themselves originated in India. It seems equally likely, however, that they took their inspiration from the watchtowers built in Han-era China and known from clay models left in tombs. Whatever the case, they soon became distinctively Chinese, and as such went on to leave their mark on Korea, Japan, and other Asian nations.

▲ The main influence of Buddhism on Chinese architecture took the form of towerlike pagodas at Buddhist shrines, such as this white pagoda in Yunnan province.

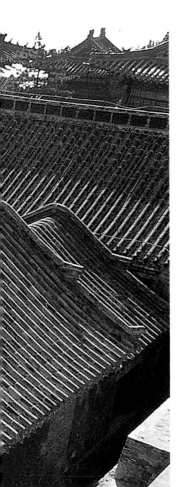

► Modeled on a Han-style town, Shuihu (Water Margin) Town was constructed as a location for a TV drama series. The site occupies approximately 90 acres (36 ha) and is laid out like a real town, complete with houses, towers, and pavilions.

The Great Wall of China

THE GREAT WALL OF CHINA IS one of the world's most famous monuments, yet some historians now prefer to talk of Great Walls (in the plural). Over the centuries several walls were built, mostly linked but following somewhat different routes and using different materials. All, however, served the same purpose: to keep the nomadic horsemen of the northern steppes, traditional enemies of the Chinese people, from raiding or invading the settled agricultural lands to the south.

History of the wall

The original Great Wall was built under the Qin on the orders of Shi Huangdi (see pages 20–21). He conscripted several hundred thousand laborers to join together existing defenses put up by the northernmost Chinese kingdoms during the Spring and Autumn and the Warring States periods. One stretch, dated to about 690 B.C.E., was identified by Chinese scientists in 2002, running for 497 miles (800 km) through southwestern Henan province.

Much of Shi Huangdi's fortification lay several hundred miles north of the wall that visitors see today, at least in its eastern section, which ended on the Liaodong Peninsula close to modern North Korea. Sections of this ancient barrier still survive in the form of a low earthen ridge, but in its day the wall was 32 feet (10 m) tall and guarded by watchtowers along its length. In total it probably ran for about 1,400 miles (2,250 km). The work, which was supervised by a general named Meng Tian, was completed in just seven years.

▲ The Jiayuguan Pass (gate), with its three-story castle, lies at the west end of the Great Wall and was built during the Ming Dynasty.

▼ The East Gate of Shanhaiguan Pass, which marks the eastern limit of the Great Wall and is known as the "First Pass under Heaven." The wall here is about 38 feet (11.6 m) high and 32 feet (10 m) wide.

Later rulers strengthened and lengthened this defensive line. Under the Han (see pages 22–23) it gave vital protection in the long wars against the Xiongnu nomads, known in the West as the Huns. The wall was extended at this time into the desert regions of Central Asia, where it provided protection for merchants and travelers using the newly opened Silk Road to Afghanistan. In 607 the Sui emperor Yangdi sent a reported 1.2 million men to rebuild and enlarge the wall. Half are said to have died of exhaustion and disease in the two years it took to complete the job.

The wall that stands today, however, was largely the work of the Ming emperors, who between the late 14th and early 17th centuries reconstructed and partly rerouted the existing defenses, as always to prevent raids by the Mongol and Turkic tribes living in the lands to the north. The Ming wall was the first to be faced with stone along much of its length. The usual method of construction was to set large blocks in parallel furrows, then to ram earth or clay into the space between. The builders used locally available materials, so that near Beijing the wall is made from quarried limestone blocks, while farther west granite or fired bricks were used instead.

A formidable barrier

In its present form the wall stretches for 3,946 miles (6,350 km) from the Yellow Sea east of Beijing to Lop Nur in the Xinjiang region of Central Asia. Originally it was guarded by watchtowers 40 feet (12 m) high, erected every few hundred yards along its length. Barracks for the troops who garrisoned the wall were built at greater intervals. Originally the guardhouses were said to be positioned two arrowlengths apart, so that no point on the wall was beyond the reach of a sentry with a crossbow. By Ming times muskets were coming into use, and many of the towers that survive today have gunports.

The Great Wall was never an impregnable defense, as China's recurrent problems with the steppe nomads show. Yet at times when the empire was strong and the fortifications were properly manned, it constituted a formidable obstacle. At all times, too, it served as a psychological barrier, demarcating Inner China from the threatening outside world that lay beyond the Middle Kingdom's borders.

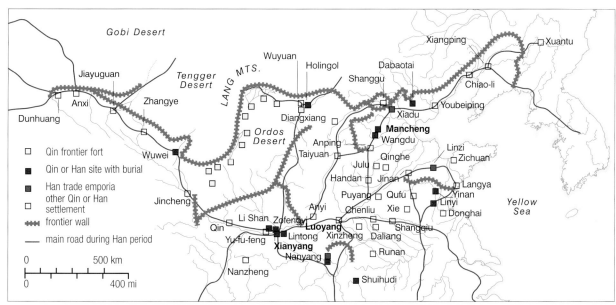

Gobi Desert

Xiangping   □ Xuantu

Wuyuan   Holingol   Dabaotai
Jiayuguan   Tengger   Shanggu   Chiao-li
Desert   LANG MTS.
Anxi   Zhangye   Dianxiang   Xiadu   □ Youbeiping
Dunhuang
Ordos   Mancheng
Desert   Wangdu
Anping   Linzi
□ Qin frontier fort   Wuwei   Taiyuan   Qinghe   Zichuan
Julu
■ Qin or Han site with burial   Handan   Jinan   Langya
Yinan
▣ Han trade emporia   Puyang   Qufu   Linyi   Yellow
other Qin or Han   Anyi   Chenliu   Xie   Donghai   Sea
□ settlement   Jincheng
✛✛✛ frontier wall   Li Shan   Zofengyi   Luoyang   Shangqiu
Qin   Lintong   Xinzheng   Daliang
— main road during Han period   Yu-fu-feng   Xianyang
Nanyang   □ Runan
0   500 km   Nanzheng
0   400 mi   ■ Shuihudi

▲ Snaking across mountains, deserts, and plateaus, the Great Wall stretches for about 3,946 miles (6,350 km) through northern China.

◄ Map of the Great Wall at the time of the Qin and Han Empires. In reality, the Great Wall was a series of frontier walls. The wall seen today near Beijing (see map on page 46) is the work of the Ming Empire and was built of solid stone.

Country Life

FROM EARLY TIMES, SETTLED AGRICULTURE was the main prop of Chinese life and the feature that most obviously distinguished the Chinese from the nomadic neighbors whom they considered "barbarians." Farmers had high status in the Confucian order of things, ranked second to scholars but ahead of artisans or merchants.

Until recent times peasants made up 90 percent or more of the nation's population (as recently as 1985 the figure was still higher than 70 percent). Yet the reality of their daily life was harsh. One reason lay in the sheer number of people exploiting a land that had been densely settled for millennia. The average size of holdings was small—in some parts of the nation no more than 4 or 5 acres (1.5–2 ha). Families could only scrape a living from such tiny plots by intensive techniques, and the annual harvest was very variable. One consequence of the shortage of available space was a lack of large farm animals, at least in crowded Inner China. There were few cattle, sheep, or horses, because there was not enough land to graze them on. People made do instead with farmyard scavengers like pigs, ducks, and chickens.

Taxes and duties

Records going back to Han times detail the hard lot of the peasant farmers, who had to struggle ceaselessly to stay ahead of their creditors. Under Wudi in the first century B.C.E., government tax collectors demanded one-fifteenth of each farm's produce, plus an additional amount for every individual in the household. The state also commandeered each farmer into one month's unpaid forced-labor duties each year, and there was always the risk of call-up for compulsory military service.

Those who fell behind with their obligations faced terrible choices: borrowing money at interest rates of up to 200 percent, selling their possessions at giveaway prices, or even having to sell their children into slavery. Small wonder, then, that one contemporary chronicler noted that "All year around they cannot afford to take even a day's rest."

Over the succeeding centuries many attempts were made to improve the peasants' condition, with mixed results. The institution of slavery died out, but serfdom, which tied landless laborers to a landowner's service, flourished. Technological advances, from the introduction of iron implements in Han times to the importation of new strains of rice (see pages 54–55) under the Song, made farms more productive. Reformers down the ages, from the Han

usurper Wang Mang to the Song minister Wang Anshi (see pages 22–23 and 38–39), sought to impose fairer systems of land distribution. Wang Anshi also provided low-interest government loans to tide farmers over the difficult months before the harvest was brought in. Yet the big landowners regularly opposed such reforms, and for the most part were able to undermine them.

In practice, a cycle developed with regard to land tenure. Owner–farmers generally flourished when the central government was strong, and the state in turn benefited from the plentiful tax revenues that they supplied. In troubled times, though, peasants looked for support to the landowners, who gave them the seeds and tools they needed to make a living in return for the bulk of their crops, often leaving the government with little or nothing.

Even so, there were worse times for the peasantry than these relapses into feudalism. These were the periods of anarchy when rural discontent erupted in peasant revolts, among them the uprising of the Yellow Turbans in 184 C.E. and

▼ Despite rapid urbanization, more than half of China's population still lives in rural areas. Most farmers work on smallholdings, and many supplement their diet with fish. Here a fisherwoman uses a traditional fishing method of using cormorants to dive into the river to catch fish.

▲ Early Chinese laborers used a yoke (a stick resting across the back of the shoulders) for carrying things. Buckets or objects were tied to the ends of the yoke. Many workers in rural areas of China continue to use a yoke to carry heavy items.

▶ As it was in historic times, planting is still often done by hand. Here a farmer sows seed using an ox-drawn plow.

the many local rebellions that preceded the downfall of the Ming in the 17th century (see pages 48–49).

Terrible though they were, such outbreaks were isolated irruptions in a generally placid scene. For most of China's long history, the story was one of quiet but constant labor. The results could be seen in the country's booming demography. China became the most populous nation in the world, and it remains so to this day largely thanks to the steady productivity of its farmers.

Ceramics and Pottery

CERAMIC PRODUCTION IN CHINA CAN BE traced back to the New Stone Age. As early as the fifth millennium B.C.E. the Neolithic village of Banpo had six separate kilns producing a red-painted ware that was handcrafted from coils of clay. By the Longshan period 2,000 years later, craftsmen were using the potter's wheel to fashion elegant cups, jars, and lidded boxes that were as thin as eggshell—all finished with a glossy black glaze.

Terra-cotta and porcelain

The Qin and Han periods are noted for their realistic earthenware models, of which the First Emperor's terra-cotta soldiers are outstanding examples (see pages 62–63). Much that is known about Han society comes from the small ceramic sculptures of buildings and their inhabitants that were found in the tombs of wealthy individuals. This tradition continued under the Tang—figures of dancers and horses, some almost 3 feet (1 m) tall, are among the most celebrated surviving artworks of the time.

Porcelain was discovered under the Han, but it was in Tang times that it was first produced on a large scale. The secret ingredient of this hard, thin, almost translucent pottery was kaolin, also known as china clay. Easily molded and with a fine texture, kaolin turned white when fired.

Porcelain manufacture reached an early peak under the Song emperors (see pages 38–39). The works of the Song potters are prized for their graceful lines and simple designs, free of unnecessary ornament. Much of the best work had a plain white glaze, although the grayish-green ware known as celadon was also characteristic of the period. Chinese potters were by now speeding up production by stacking their vessels for firing in protective racks called saggars. The growing popularity of tea drinking produced a fresh market for porcelain vessels, which largely replaced earthenware from this time on.

Official ware and Ming china

The founding of imperial potteries patronized by the nation's rulers was another innovation of Song times. Early in the 12th century the artist–emperor Huizong set up the first imperial pottery in his capital Kaifeng. Its products were known as *kuan* ("official") ware, and they remain among the most highly valued examples of the Chinese potters' art.

The disruption caused by the Jürchen and Mongol irruptions into northern China drove many potters south, and by the time the Ming Dynasty was established in 1344, the bulk of production had shifted below the Yangtze (Chang) River. A new imperial pottery was established in 1369 at Jingdezhen in Jiangxi province, in a region rich in china-clay deposits. Jingdezhen would remain the main focus of the porcelain industry for the rest of the imperial period.

Production at Jingdezhen was supervised by a court eunuch dispatched from Beijing. Skilled craftsmen painted designs onto objects shaped out of a thick paste of powdered stone and kaolin, and the finished work was then

▲ Realistic earthenware towers and other architectural models were popular during the Han Dynasty. They were placed inside the tombs of wealthy individuals in order to accompany the deceased into the afterlife.

◀ A small dish from the Ming Dynasty (c.1500), with the characteristic blue and white decoration. In the center are a spotted deer and a crane (symbols of longevity) against a background of pine, cherry, and bamboo (plants of good omen that herald the spring).

glazed and fired. Yet few if any of the pieces were the product of a single artist, for the factory operated a production-line system: each individual artisan specialized in some small part of the total design, passing the piece to others to sketch in the remaining details. The final touch was provided by a calligrapher, who added a pottery mark and a date to authenticate the vessel.

The best-known produce of the Jingdezhen factory was the blue and white ware still indelibly associated with the Ming name. The blue coloration came from cobalt that reached China from Persia along the Silk Road (see pages 26–27); the Chinese called it "Muslim Blue" because of its place of origin.

It was in the Ming era that Chinese pottery first found its way to the West in large quantities, carried by the Portuguese merchants established in Macao. In time the word "china" would become synonymous with porcelain in English-speaking countries. More than any other objects, Ming cups and vases served to introduce the nation's culture to a new world beyond the seas.

▲ A pair of sculpted horses and riders from the Tang Dynasty. Under the Tang, China was a cosmopolitan and tolerant nation that allowed literature, painting, and the ceramic arts to flourish. Tang potters introduced several new techniques, including the use of three-colored glazes.

Theater and Opera

I N THE CHINESE TRADITION THEATER AND opera are one and the same, since classical drama combines music, dance, mime, and acrobatics as well as the spoken word. Its deepest roots have been traced back to the antics of the *wu* priests, magicians who performed dances in the course of invoking and exorcising spirits (see pages 56–57). Although originally religious in nature, their performances were later staged for entertainment.

By Tang times, a courtly dramatic tradition had developed. One patron was Emperor Xuanzong (712–756), who established a school for singers and musicians known as the Pear Garden. (Actors in China are still called "children of the Pear Garden.") Their most ambitious performances celebrated military victories in dance, music, and song. One such production, *Breaking the Battle Line*, featured 128 boys wearing silver armor and carrying lances. Short, two-character sketches featuring stock characters were also popular at court.

New drama

The emergence of drama as a serious art form, however, dates from the period of Mongol rule (see pages 42–43). China's scholars were deprived of their normal livelihood in the bureaucracy and had to find fresh outlets for their talents. At the same time, the old courtly audience was dispersed, and the civil-service examination system came to a temporary halt, loosening the grip of the Confucian classics on

▶ Traditional Chinese drama has four role types: *Shan*, *Dan*, *Jin*, and *Chou*. This actor is playing the part of a *Jin* (a male character with a strong personality). Every *Jin* character has a unique pattern painted on his face, signifying his personality, age, and temperament.

▼ Theatrical characters in traditional Chinese costume. As well as being performed in theaters, plays were put on at parties and festivals, to celebrate harvest time, and to mark the birthdays of deities. Many of the themes of the plays were taken from history, religious stories, or folk tales.

the nation's intellectual life. It was a time for experiment that also saw the rise of the novel.

The earliest center of the new drama was Beijing, although from 1280 it was replaced by the southern city of Hangzhou. The plays, mostly four acts long, were different from anything that had gone before. To start with, they used a language that was not very different from everyday speech. They took their plots from Chinese history or from Daoist or Buddhist legend, and featured well-loved themes such as an individual's triumph over official injustice, the virtue of loyalty, or the destructive power of sexual passion. The action was regularly interrupted by arias, sung to popular tunes that were familiar to the audiences.

The theatrical tradition that developed under the Mongols continued and expanded in the Ming era. What emerged was a highly stylized form of theater in which the dramatic action was choreographed to music, played by an orchestra that occupied a corner of the stage. Set-piece dance interludes climaxed in spectacular acrobatic sequences representing conflict or war. Convention demanded that only men could appear on the stage, so all the women's parts were played by female impersonators. There was no scenery, no curtains, and very few props.

Face paint and body movement

Most of the visual interest was provided by rich costumes and heavy make-up, designed to show the key features of each character at a glance. Villains, for instance, had their faces painted white, while generals and other military men appeared in fierce shades of red, yellow, and black. The actors used stylized gestures to indicate familiar actions such as swimming, walking up- or downstairs, opening and closing doors, or climbing into a carriage. A character carrying a whip was instantly understood to be on horseback until he raised a leg, signifying that he was dismounting. People dressed in black were invisible, while someone with a horsehair switch (thin whip) represented a spirit or ghost.

The tradition established under the Yuan and Ming proved exceptionally durable. Until recent times the " 100 Plays of the Yuan Dynasty" formed the basis of the nation's dramatic repertory, so familiar to theater-goers that they knew most of the plots and many of the songs by heart. Although new, Western-influenced forms of entertainment have largely supplemented the traditional theater in recent years, the old plays are still performed and remain an essential part of China's cultural heritage.

Science and Technology

CHINA WAS IN THE FOREFRONT OF technological development from early times. Even before the First Emperor's day, Chinese warriors were fighting with crossbows, which were not used in the West for another 1,500 years. Harnesses for horses were already in use, and possibly stirrups as well. There was also a long tradition of studying the heavens. Evidence from oracle bones shows that Chinese astronomers had established a calendar of 365¼ days by the 14th century B.C.E., and they observed the passage of Halley's Comet as early as 240 B.C.E.

Han technology

The explosion of invention during the Han years could hardly have been predicted. Innovations of that time ranged from the suspension bridge and the sternpost rudder (first known from a model boat found in a Former Han tomb) to the wheelbarrow (the "wooden ox," first recorded in the first century B.C.E.). Engineers channeled natural gas through pipes for use as fuel, and made seesawlike devices to drive drill bits that cut boreholes in salt mines almost 1 mile (1,500 m) deep. Scientists observed sunspots and developed a lodestone compass with a spoon-shaped needle—the "south-pointer." This device was mostly used at the time by Daoist priests checking for sites for religious rituals.

The first recorded seismograph—an instrument for detecting earthquakes—also dates from Han times.

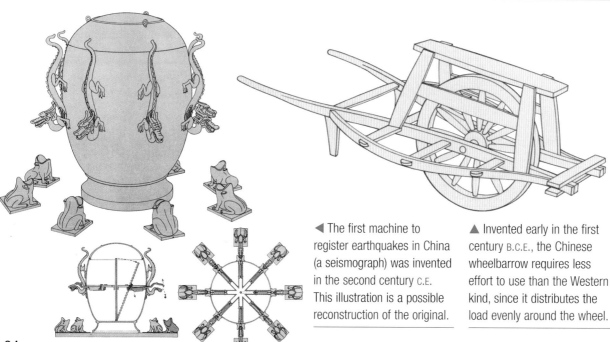

▲ A reconstruction of a hydraulic clockwork mechanism built in the 11th century C.E. The mechanism powered a celestial globe (second floor) and an armillary sphere (on the roof).

◄ The first machine to register earthquakes in China (a seismograph) was invented in the second century C.E. This illustration is a possible reconstruction of the original.

▲ Invented early in the first century B.C.E., the Chinese wheelbarrow requires less effort to use than the Western kind, since it distributes the load evenly around the wheel.

▲ The Chinese first invented movable-type printing in the 11th century, but the Koreans later developed it to high levels of sophistication. A Korean was head of the Chinese Imperial Printing office in 1777, when this picture was made. It shows printers working on a collection of rare books.

Made by Zhang Heng in 132 C.E., it indicated the presence and direction of earthquakes by releasing a ball from the mouth of a bronze dragon into the gaping mouth of one of eight toads stationed around its base. Zhang also devised an armillary sphere to trace the movements of the planets.

China's inventive zeal survived the disruption of the Six Dynasties period; in the relatively unscathed south there were even technological innovations at the time, including the use of blast furnaces to produce high-grade steel. Yet it took the restoration of peace and unity under the Tang Dynasty to regain something of the momentum of the Han years. Novelties of the Tang era included the use of fingerprints for identification and the application of whale and seal oil for waterproofing.

Paper, print, and technological progress

The most important advances of the Tang years were in the field of printing. Paper itself was a Chinese invention, dating back to the Former Han epoch (see pages 64–65). It came into its own as a medium for transmitting ideas with the development of woodblock printing under the Tang from the eighth century on. Once carved on a block, the characters making up a single page of text could be inked and reproduced many times. This method of replication proved more suitable to the needs of the Chinese language, with its thousands of separate characters, than movable-type printing, also invented in China in the 1040s. The woodblock technique was used at first to stamp out single sheets, but was soon applied to books—the earliest known example, a Buddhist text found in a cave at Dunhuang, dates from 868.

By Song times, the tide of technological progress had become strong enough to cause something approaching an industrial revolution. In the textile business, large-scale plants produced bulk goods with the aid of silk-reeling machines and new types of spinning wheel. Produce was shipped in ocean-going vessels equipped with compasses, now put to use for navigation. Armament manufacturers had a new substance at their disposal—the first text containing a formula for gunpowder dates from 1044.

If the industrial revolution was never truly realized, it was in part because science was less highly regarded in China than literary and philosophical learning. The merchants who put technology to use had lower status than the scholars who formed government policy, and science was never admitted to the civil service exam curriculum.

▶ This treadle-operated silk-reeling machine rapidly drew threads of silk from several silkworm cocoons. The threads passed a ramping arm (left-hand side), which shifted the eyelets through which the fibers passed, laying them down in broad bands on a rotating reeling frame (right-hand side).

The Forbidden City

FROM THE EARLY MING ERA ON, CHINA WAS ruled from inside a walled complex that lay at the heart of Beijing. Known literally as the Purple Forbidden City, it was a world to itself, with elaborate rules and rituals. For the emperors' subjects, the imperial court that it sheltered was the hub of the Middle Kingdom and so, by extension, of the entire civilized world.

The idea of such a palace complex was not new. When the Ming emperor Yongle decided to build the Forbidden City soon after moving the capital from Nanjing (see pages 44–45), he replicated an earlier enclave that had risen in the Tang capital Changan 600 years before. Made up of 250 acres (100 ha) of palaces, temples, and ceremonial halls, it was a city

within a city within another city. Beyond its own walls lay the Imperial City, an enclosure 1,500 acres (600 ha) in extent where officials serving the emperor lived and worked. Both the Forbidden and Imperial cities formed part of Beijing's Inner City, which had a perimeter wall 15 miles (24 km) long.

The Forbidden City itself took the form of a classic Chinese household or temple enclosure on a gigantic scale. Following a well-established pattern (see pages 74–75), it had a rectangular ground plan oriented on a north–south axis and constructed around a series of courtyards. Three of its entrance gates—those to the south (Meridian Gate), east, and west—opened onto the Outer Court, the public part of the complex where those who had business with the emperor were admitted. The fourth, northern, gate (Gate of Divine Might) was for use by the emperor and his immediate household only. It gave access to the Inner Court, a private area that was walled off from the rest of the Forbidden City. This sanctum was restricted to the emperor, his immediate family, and his concubines, together with the eunuchs who served them.

▼ Surrounded by a high wall and a deep moat, the Forbidden City had approximately 800 buildings. The most important royal and government buildings are shown on the plan below.

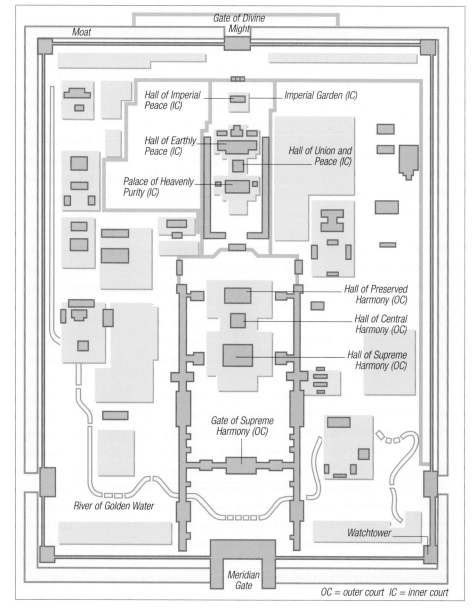

Gate of Divine Might

Moat

Hall of Imperial Peace (IC)

Imperial Garden (IC)

Hall of Earthly Peace (IC)

Hall of Union and Peace (IC)

Palace of Heavenly Purity (IC)

Hall of Preserved Harmony (OC)

Hall of Central Harmony (OC)

Hall of Supreme Harmony (OC)

Gate of Supreme Harmony (OC)

River of Golden Water

Watchtower

Meridian Gate

OC = outer court IC = inner court

▲ In China yellow symbolizes royalty and is a dominant color among the buildings of the Forbidden City, particularly the roofs. The red used for many of the walls represents happiness and luck.

Three halls of harmony

An ancient formula dating back to Zhou times proclaimed that the Son of Heaven (the emperor) should rule from "three courts." The Outer Court had as its central feature three vast audience halls set one behind the other along the central axis. The greatest was the Hall of Supreme Harmony, where the emperor formally received visitors, who were expected to express respect by "kowtowing"—kneeling on all fours and touching their forehead

to the floor. The smaller Hall of Central Harmony was a waiting chamber where the emperor rested before the start of public audiences, while the Hall of Preserved Harmony was used for state banquets and, latterly, as the place where the last round of civil service examinations took place in the presence of the emperor himself (see pages 70–71). Dozens of other structures surrounded the three halls, including the imperial library, ceremonial gateways, and servants' quarters, warehouses, and storerooms.

In its entirety the Forbidden City encompassed some 800 buildings with more than 8,000 rooms. It was so large that parts of it were deserted, sometimes for long periods. One 19th-century visitor described finding an entire abandoned courtyard; none of the palace officials could remember why it was disused.

The Forbidden City symbolized the grandeur of the Chinese emperors, but it also represented their remoteness from the people they governed. Visitors had to kneel at its gates to gain admission. Within its walls, the rulers moved in an insulated world, surrounded by fawning officials, concubines, and eunuchs. Today it is a monument to a vanished era, listed by UNESCO as the world's largest grouping of ancient wooden buildings and open to everyone as the Palace Museum.

◀ The Forbidden City was home to 24 emperors (14 Ming and 10 Qing) and was the center of the kingdom for almost 500 years. Today it houses more than 900,000 priceless antiques preserved from dynasties throughout Chinese history. The large building at right is the Hall of Supreme Harmony.

▼ The Hall of Supreme Harmony (the throne hall) was used for ceremonies such as the emperor's birthday, on the occasion of dispatching generals to battle, and for receiving visitors.

Rivers and Canals

CHINESE CIVILIZATION GREW UP AROUND great rivers. The first dynasties came to power on the middle reaches of the Yellow (Huang) River, where the nutrient-rich loess soil was easy to work and produced rich crops. The earliest rice-growing cultures sprang up in the hotter, wetter lands of the Yangtze (Chang) Delta (see pages 54–55).

Yet the various parts of the country were very differently supplied with rainfall. The south has always been well watered, but precipitation in the north is much more variable, making the region more liable to cycles of drought and flooding. Even so, northerners are better provided than most of the inhabitants of Outer China, where rain can be scarce or even—as in the Takla Makan Desert of Central Asia or Mongolia's Gobi—almost entirely absent.

"In the north take a horse; in the south, go by boat" was ancient advice for Chinese travelers. In the drier northern regions, which were less well provided with rivers, most transportation was by land. The

▶ Efficient inland water transportation boosted the economy under the Song emperors. Heavily laden barges and junks are shown on the river in this view of Kaifeng (capital of Song China) from about 1200.

▼ This map shows mainly the canal system of the Ming period. The system, begun by the Sui emperors, linked the vital grain-producing Yangtze (Chang) Delta region with the political center of the empire and the northern border zone.

roads were crowded not just with people on horseback or on foot but also with ox carts carrying goods and litters bearing high officials on their business. In stark contrast, southern China was criss-crossed by waterways that were clogged with barges. Some boats had sails of bamboo or reed matting, while rowers propelled others using fishtail-shaped oars. The relative absence of roads even had strategic significance, making it harder for the mounted nomads who regularly invaded northern China to penetrate the southern areas.

From early on engineers sought to supplement the river network by building canals. One of the first great projects, dating back to 487 B.C.E., connected the Yellow and Huai Rivers. Hundreds of miles downstream the Huai was similarly joined to the Yangtze, thereby providing a direct link between China's two greatest river systems. Three hundred and fifty years later a Han emperor linked his capital of Changan directly to the Yellow River, cutting out the need to use the unreliable Wei River.

The Grand Canal

The greatest of all the nation's artificial waterways was the Grand Canal, built on the orders of the Sui emperor Yangdi and completed in 610 C.E. Its construction helped fill a gap in the empire's existing communication network, namely the lack of a north–south artery. (All the great rivers ran from west to east, draining into the Yellow/China Sea.)

Beijing

Liaodong Peninsula

Yellow (Huang) before 603 B.C.E.

Bo Hai

Yellow (Huang) after 603 B.C.E.

Shandong Peninsula

Yellow (Huang)

Grand Canal

Yellow Sea

Grand Canal

Huai

Huai

Yangtze

Yangtze (Chang)

Hangzhou

— ancient course of Yellow (Huang) River
☐ ancient coastline
▪▪▪▪ canal

0 ___ 200 km
0 ___ 150 mi

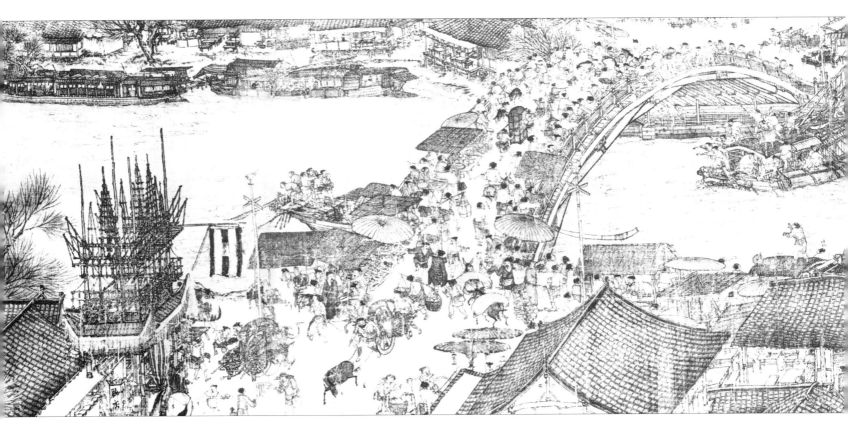

The canal, which combined newly built sections and existing waterways, linked the southern port of Hangzhou with Beijing in the north by way of Yangdi's capital, Luoyang (see map on page 33). Later dynasties added to Yangdi's work, and under the Ming an entirely new arm was cut through central China to shorten journey times to Beijing, by then the emperors' seat of government.

Known to generations of Chinese as the River of Transportation, the Grand Canal from the start played a central part in the nation's life. Its great function was to carry grain from the southern rice lands northward to the cities of the North China Plain. Importantly, it also supplied the armies stationed in the sensitive northeastern border region. One Ming observer called the canal the nation's throat, claiming that Beijing would starve if it failed to supply rice even for a day. Yet the barges that crowded its waters did not just carry grain; private craft also used it, making it a vital artery of general trade. Knowing its economic and strategic significance, the authorities took care to maintain it. By one estimate, up to 150,000 soldiers crewed the grain fleets, while the labor of many more civilians went to dredge and maintain its channels.

Stretching for more than 1,100 miles (1,800 km), the Grand Canal remains in use today. So too are many other waterways. A recent estimate suggests the network covers 68,000 miles (110,000 km) and carries more than 400 million tonnes of cargo a year.

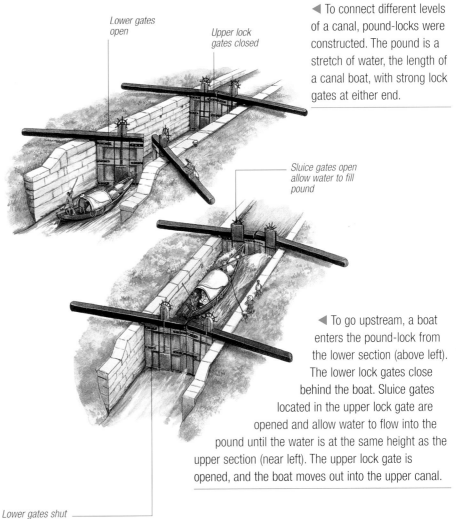

Lower gates open

Upper lock gates closed

Sluice gates open allow water to fill pound

Lower gates shut

◄ To connect different levels of a canal, pound-locks were constructed. The pound is a stretch of water, the length of a canal boat, with strong lock gates at either end.

◄ To go upstream, a boat enters the pound-lock from the lower section (above left). The lower lock gates close behind the boat. Sluice gates located in the upper lock gate are opened and allow water to flow into the pound until the water is at the same height as the upper section (near left). The upper lock gate is opened, and the boat moves out into the upper canal.

Festivals

CHINA'S FESTIVALS PROVIDE A LIVING LINK with the nation's past. Like such Western equivalents as Christmas and Thanksgiving, they are special occasions that offer a break from the normal working routine and bring families together. In addition, they provide an excuse for noisy, colorful festivities enlivened by firecrackers, incense smoke, sporting competitions, and parades.

Chinese New Year

The festivities are mostly linked to the lunar months (28 days), so they fall on different dates each year. The Spring Festival, known in the West as Chinese New Year, can take place any time from late January to the end of February. Traditionally minded families make offerings to Zao Jun, the Daoist Kitchen God

▶ Fireworks feature in many Chinese festivals. The Chinese were probably the first to invent gunpowder, and it was soon used to make firecrackers. The loud sounds were considered good for chasing away evil spirits and celebrating victory in battle.

▲ Dragon boats race across the water during the Dragon Boat Festival in Hong Kong. The festival commemorates the drowning of the poet Qu Yuan.

whose image hangs in many homes. Each year at this time Zao supposedly goes to heaven to report on the behavior of individual family members over the previous 12 months. Prudent householders seek to win his favor by providing offerings of sticky candies and rice (so his lips might be sealed) or by burning his image in alcohol—considered equivalent to offering the spirit a drink. At the festival's end they pin up a fresh image of the god to keep watch on the household through the coming year.

The mood of the three-day public holiday is one of spring cleaning, marking a fresh start at a time when nature itself is being renewed. Before the break begins, people clean their homes, settle their debts, get their hair cut, and buy new clothes. Shoppers buy candies and toys for their children and presents for relatives and friends. Some hang red scrolls from their front doors, wishing for luck in the coming year. On the festival's eve families stay up until midnight to let off firecrackers, then spend the next three days visiting friends and relatives, exchanging gifts, and feasting on special dishes—*jiaozi* steamed dumplings in the north, and a sweet rice pudding called *nian gao* in the south.

Honoring the dead

◀ A group of drummers celebrate Chinese New Year in a street parade in Hong Kong. Today New Year festivities take place in Chinese communities all over the world and often last for several days.

Rooted in Confucian ideas of ancestor worship, the Qing Ming festival, celebrated in April, is a time to remember the dead. Families go to cemeteries to tidy the graves of departed loved ones. Some burn imitation money, supposedly transferring its use to needy relations in the spirit world.

Also in April or early May, people in coastal regions honor Tian Hou (Tin Hau in Cantonese).

These festivities celebrate Mo Niang, a fisherman's daughter in 11th-century Fukien, who could apparently predict storms. Waking one night from a dream that her father and brothers were in peril at sea, she rushed to the shore and magically calmed the waters so that the family boat returned safely even though many other men drowned. Renamed Tian Hou ("Queen of Heaven"), Mo duly became the patron of seafarers everywhere, and her image is paraded today through the streets of Hong Kong and other ports to the sound of cymbals and firecrackers.

The Dragon Boat Festival, usually held in June, commemorates the poet Qu Yuan (see pages 72–73), who drowned himself in the Milo River to protest against the political corruption of the Warring States era (see pages 16–17). The local people were so devastated by the loss of the poet that they beat the water with paddles to scare the fishes away from his corpse. Now the event is celebrated annually with boat races between vessels decorated with pennants and bearing dragon masks for figureheads.

Second only to the Spring Festival as a family celebration is the Zhonq Qiu, or Mid-Autumn Festival, falling in late September or early October. It honors the moon. Young and old alike eat mooncakes—circular pastries stuffed with nuts, dried fruit, and sometimes marinated beef or pork—and go out into the chilly night bearing lanterns designed in fantastic shapes, lit from within by candles. The sight of thousands of tiny lights moving over darkened hillsides has added a touch of poetry to millions of Chinese childhoods, helping explain why this and other festivals are still celebrated even at a time when few believe in the gods they once honored.

91

Glossary

acupuncture
Traditional therapy that involves puncturing the skin with needles to cure disease and relieve pain.

ancestor worship
The ancient Chinese custom of honoring dead relatives in the hope that they will intercede for the living in the spirit world.

animism
Belief that the natural world is populated by gods and spirits.

bodhisattva
In the Buddhist religion, a saintly being who voluntarily delays his or her own attainment of the paradisal state of nirvana to help other people attain salvation.

calligraphy
Handwriting practiced as a fine art.

Confucianism
The doctrines associated with the philosopher Kongfuzi, or Confucius, He emphasized respect for order and social responsibility.

Daoism
Initially a philosophical system based on the notion of blending the individual personality into the flow of the universe and of nature, Daoism developed into a popular religion devoted to the worship of China's ancient gods.

feng shui
Ancient Daoist system purporting to study the flow of *qi*, or energy, through the landscape.

feudal system
A social order in which lords protect and maintain their vassals (tenants) in return for specified services including military support in time of war.

fief
The estate provided by a feudal overlord to a vassal (tenant).

Forbidden City
The imperial enclave at the heart of Beijing where Chinese emperors lived and reigned from the early years of the Ming Dynasty on.

geomancy
In China, the study of the hidden force of *qi* (energy) at work in the landscape as practiced by followers of feng shui.

Grand Canal
Waterway originally built under the Sui Dynasty to link the rice lands of southern China with Beijing and the North China Plain.

Han Chinese
The majority ethnic group of Inner China, today comprising more than 90 percent of the population. The name comes from the Han Dynasty.

Huang Di
Literally "the Yellow Emperor," a legendary early ruler claimed to have introduced the arts of civilization to the nation.

Hundred Schools
Traditional name for the wealth of different doctrines propounded by philosophers in the troubled Warring States period. Both Daoism and Confucianism emerged from this time of intellectual ferment.

jade
A semiprecious stone, composed either of jadeite or nephrite and occurring in a range of shades from green to white, which was highly prized in ancient China and remains so today.

Jürchen
Nomadic people of Manchuria who seized northern China from the Song Dynasty in 1122. The Manchus, who established their own dynasty in 1644, were descendants of the Jürchen.

Koguryo
Powerful and long-lasting state, founded on the borders of Korea and Manchuria in the 1st century B.C.E. It survived until the 7th century C.E.

legalism
Totalitarian doctrine, developed in the Hundred Schools era of Chinese philosophy, that was espoused by the First Emperor. It subordinated the rights of the individual to the demands of the state.

li
Key concept, most often translated as "propriety," that defined Confucius's view of the right form of social conduct. Implying a proper respect for one's moral and social obligations, the term was also used for the rites through which such duties were expressed.

loess
Grainy, wind-blown soil, a mixture of clay and silt particles, found in the middle reaches of the Yellow (Huang) River Valley.

Longshan Culture
Early Chinese cultural period that saw the development of trade and the first appearance of towns.

Manchuria
Region bordering China to the northeast beyond the Great Wall that eventually became joined to the nation when Manchu rulers seized power from the Ming Dynasty in 1644.

meridians
In acupuncture, the term applied to the invisible channels believed to conduct the life force *qi* through the human body. The acupuncture points where needles are inserted are positioned along the meridians.

Middle Kingdom
Name that the Chinese have given their own state since Shang times, reflecting the view that China is the center of the civilized world.

Nanchao
Thai kingdom established in what is now the Chinese province of Yunnan in about the year 600 C.E. It was conquered by Kublai Khan's Mongol forces in 1253 and later united with China.

neolithic
Relating to the New Stone Age— the final period of the Stone Age that saw the transition from hunter-gathering to farming.

oracle bones
Animal bones bearing inscriptions made by court diviners who used the bones to foretell the future. The inscriptions are the earliest form of Chinese writing and an essential source for the nation's prehistory.

paddy
Field saturated with water to a depth of 2–4 inches (5–10 cm) and used for the cultivation of rice.

pagoda
Multistoried tower with overhanging eaves, typically with each story marginally smaller than the one below. Usually associated with Buddhist temples.

qi
Fundamental concept of Chinese medicine, sometimes translated as "air" or "breath," that describes the force or energy animating all life. *Qi* circulates around the body through the meridians.

Qidans
Also known as Khitans. An originally nomadic steppe people inhabiting the north part of the Manchurian plain who established the kingdom of Liao on China's northeastern border in the time of troubles following the collapse of the Tang Dynasty.

Red Turbans
Peasant rebels who took up arms against the Mongol Yuan Dynasty, in part inspired by the messianic views of the White Lotus sect.

shamanism
Folk religion centered on inspired individuals—shamans—who claim to be able to contact the spirit world in a trance state induced by taking drugs or through ecstatic dancing. Shamans typically claim healing or prophetic powers.

shi
Class of educated retainers in the service of kings and high noblemen of the Warring States period.

Silk Road
Trade route stretching from western China through Afghanistan and Uzbekistan to Iran and on to the Middle East.

Sinicization
The adoption of Chinese ways, as practiced by some neighboring peoples.

Son of Heaven
A title accorded to the rulers of China from early times, recalling ancient beliefs in their divine ancestry.

Spring and Autumn period
The name traditionally given to the first part of the Eastern Zhou

period, from 771 to 481 B.C.E. It comes from the *Spring and Autumn Annals*, a chronicle recording events in the eastern state of Lu between 722 and 481.

Tanguts
Nomadic people of Tibetan origin who founded the kingdom of Xixia on China's northwestern border in the time of troubles following the collapse of the Tang Dynasty.

Tarim Basin
Desert region on the Silk Road, now in China's far western region of Xinjiang.

Tatars
Also known as Tartars. The name of a branch of the Mongol people living south of the Amur River in Inner Mongolia, who were defeated by the Yongle Emperor in the early 15th century. Early European writers, including Marco Polo, used the word "Tartar" to describe all Mongols.

Warring States era
The latter part of the Eastern Zhou epoch, from 481 to 221 B.C.E. So called because China was divided between a number of rival, semi-independent kingdoms, struggling for supremacy with one another while offering nominal allegiance to the Eastern Zhou rulers.

White Lotus
A banned religious group, drawing its ideas from both Buddhism and Daoism, that promised the return of a Messiahlike figure, the Maitreya, in the latter years of the Mongol Yuan Dynasty. White Lotus devotees formed the backbone of the Red Turban rebel groups.

wu
Shamans who from deep in Chinese prehistory claimed magical powers attained in ecstatic states. In time beliefs and practices pioneered by the *wu* fed through into the rites of the Daoist religion, while their

dances may have helped inspire early Chinese theatre.

Xia Dynasty
Semilegendary dynasty that, according to ancient Chinese historical records, immediately preceded the Shang. If it existed, it would have been contemporary with the Longshan Culture. Archaeologists have recently found sites that may be associated with it.

Xiongnu
Nomadic people of the Mongolian steppes who fought a long sequence of border wars with the Chinese in Han Dynasty times and who invaded northern China after its collapse, sacking its chief cities, Luoyang (in 311) and Changan (in 316). Historians think that they are the people known in the West as the Huns.

Xixia
State founded on China's north-western border in the late 10th

century by the Tibetan Tangut people. Genghis Khan invaded it in 1207, and it was subsequently incorporated into the Mongol (Yuan) Empire.

Yangshao Culture
The earliest Chinese cultural period, distinguished by substantial farming villages and attractive pottery made from coils of clay without the benefit of the potter's wheel.

Yellow Turbans
Peasant rebels who rose in the year 184 C.E. against the Han Dynasty in its last declining years. So called from their distinctive headgear, the insurgents were inspired by Daoist religious ideas. Although the rebellion was eventually put down, it fatally weakened the Han by enabling the generals commissioned to suppress it to set up as semi-independent warlords.

FURTHER READING

Charles Benn, *China's Golden Age: Everyday Life in the Tang Dynasty* (Oxford University Press), 2004.
Caroline Blunden and Mark Elvin, *Cultural Atlas of China* (Checkmark Books), 1998.
Roberto Ciarla (ed.), *The Eternal Army* (White Star), 2005.
Arthur Cotterell, *China: A History* (Pimlico), 1995.
Maurice Cotterell, *The Terracotta Warriors* (Headline), 2003.
Patricia Buckley Ebrey and Kwang-Ching Liu, *The Cambridge Illustrated History of China* (Cambridge University Press), 1999.
John King Fairbank and Merle Goldman, *China: A New History* (Belknap Press), 1998.
Bamber and Christina Gascoigne, *The Dynasties of China* (Carroll & Graf), 2003.
Ray Huang, *1587—A Year of No Significance: The Ming Dynasty in Decline* (Yale University Press), 1982.
W. Scott Morton and Charlton M. Lewis, *China: Its History and Culture* (McGraw-Hill), 2004.
J. A. G. Roberts, *A Concise History of China* (Harvard University Press), 1999.
Jonathan Spence, *The Search for Modern China* (W. W. Norton & Co.), 2001.

Picture Books

George Beshore, *Science in Ancient China* (Franklin Watts), 1998.
Paul Challen, *Life in Ancient China* (Crabtree Publishing Co.), 2004.
Arthur Cotterell, *Ancient China* (DK Children), 2005.

Wei Jiang, *The Legend of Mu Lan: A Heroine of Ancient China* (Victory Press), 1998.
William Lindesay and Guo Baofu, *The Terracotta Army* (Odyssey Publications), 1999.
Jane O'Connor, *The Emperor's Silent Army* (Viking Juvenile), 2002.
Virginia Schomp, *The Ancient Chinese* (Franklin Watts), 2005.
Brian Williams, *Ancient China* (Viking Juvenile), 1996.
Suzanne Williams, *Made in China: Ideas and Inventions from Ancient China* (Pacific View), 1997.

Useful Web Sites

http://en.wikipedia.org/wiki/China
General information about China, including its history, culture, religion, and technological developments.

www.chaos.umd.edu/history/toc.html
A useful History of China resource provided by a graduate student at the University of Maryland.

www.fordham.edu/halsall/eastasia/eastasiasbook.html
This site, listing specialized web sites, goes under the title of the Internet East Asian History Sourcebook, collated by a historian at Fordham University, NYC.

http://orpheus.ucsd.edu/chinesehistory/othersites.html
A list of China-related web sites from the University of California San Diego campus.

Index